carl e. thoresen
michael j. mahoney

behavioral
self-control

behavioral
self-control

behavioral self-control

carl e. thoresen
Stanford University ' ' '
michael j. mahoney
Pennsylvania State University

HOLT, RINEHART AND WINSTON, INC.
New York Chicago San Francisco Atlanta
Dallas Montreal Toronto London Sydney

"Whatever liberates our spirit without giving us self-control is disastrous." Goethe

To Katherine, Fran, and Al—and to those clinical and research workers whose efforts in behavioral self-control may come to enhance individual dignity and personal freedom

BF
632
T54

Library of Congress Cataloging in Publication Data

Thoresen, Carl E.
  Behavioral self-control.

  1. Self-control. 2. Behavior modification.
I. Mahoney, Michael, joint author. II. Title.
[DNLM: 1. Behavior.   BF632   T489b   1974]
BF632.T54   153.8   73–14601
ISBN 0–03–091522–8

Foreword

Behavior theory has been undergoing major changes. For years man was viewed mainly as a respondent to environmental influences which automatically shaped and controlled his actions. On closer inspection, man proved to be more active and the environment less autonomous. Influences that were believed to affect behavior automatically, in fact, have limited impact unless consciously mediated. The manner in which environmental events are cognitively transformed, reduced, and elaborated determines what will be learned and how well it will be retained.

In causal analyses, the environment assumes an autonomous status when only one side of a two-sided process is represented. The environment is not an operator that inevitably impinges upon individuals. Rather, it is only a potentiality until actualized through appropriate actions. Fires do not burn people unless they touch them. Rewards and punishments remain in abeyance until the relevant performances occur. Through their conduct people play an active role in producing the reinforcement contingencies that impinge upon them. Thus, behavior partly creates the environment, and the environment influences the behavior in a reciprocal fashion. It is just as important to analyze how man shapes environmental conditions as it is to assess how conditions modify his actions. A distinguishing feature of man is that he is capable of creating self-regulative influences. By functioning as an agent as well as an object of influence, man has some power of self-direction.

Nothing typifies more clearly the operation of reciprocal processes than the phenomenon of self-control. In this volume, Thoresen and Mahoney present incisive analyses of self-regulative processes together with evidence bearing on the central issues. They identify the component functions and outline potentially effective means of developing self-directive skills. There is still much to be done. But this contribution is a significant beginning in the work that will eventually aid man in his quest for self-mastery.

ALBERT BANDURA

Preface

Human freedom and individual dignity are very much a function of power
—the ability to influence and the skill to change. Many things, of course,
are simply not within our power to control, but many more are than is
generally conceded by layman and professional alike. Epictetus, the ancient
Stoic philosopher, observed almost 2000 years ago that human actions—
thoughts, emotions, opinions, aversions—were within a person's power to
control, if he *believed* in such a possibility. We believe that the power to
control one's actions is within the realm of possibility. We can learn self-
control skills if we first concede such a possibility.

Despite the wisdom of Epictetus and others, we have remained essentially ignorant of *how* to control our own acts. Admonishments to "know thyself," to exert willpower, or to think positively have not sufficed. We have lacked and often denied the perspective that synthesizes the "within and without," a view that sees self-control as a function of what goes on within the person, as well as things and events without. This deficit in turn has restricted development of a technology for teaching and learning the skills of self-control.

Techniques for teaching self-control have existed for some time. *The Bhagavad-Gita*, for example, is in part a two-thousand-year-old manual of self-control techniques. But since this work has been part of a religious and philosophical system, it has not been attractive or even available to others. Today, however, due to several diverse developments such as the social-learning perspective that incorporates the "cognitive" with the "behavioral," and the physiological biofeedback experiments, a scientific technology of self-control has started to emerge.

As social-learning psychologists concerned with combining scholarly research with effective clinical practice, we offer in this text a tentative behavioral framework for self-control. Admittedly we have been forced to omit many methods relevant to the topic of self-control because of space limitations. Many techniques (e.g., self-hypnosis, autogenic training, meditation, natural birth control) merit consideration but discussion of them is available elsewhere. These strategies, however, can be conceptualized within the behavioral framework. Whether they should be is at present more a matter of personal preference, since the results of self-control methods can often be explained by a number of different theoretical rationales.

We have observed with pleasure, both within behavioral psychology and various "psychodynamic" schools of thought, the lessening of polemics associated with narrow theoretical orthodoxies that have viewed self-control as strictly an exercise of will or a disguised consequence of external forces. The key to self-control lies in understanding how internal *and* external events function together. A noted psychoanalyst, for example, has recently observed that self-control and personal freedom can be gained only by "trying harder" *and* "trying differently," that is, by changing what we think and by changing the external environment.

In organizing the text we made several decisions. After an introductory chapter, which includes a brief review of "stimulus control" methods, and a chapter on methodological techniques and problems in self-control research, chapters are presented on self-observation, self-reinforcement, self-punishment, and covert (internal) self-control methods. Unavoidable overlap exists in such a presentation. Self-observation skills in some form, for example, are a part of most self-control efforts discussed in other chapters. Yet self-observation as a method for gathering information and as a self-control technique does deserve the careful attention not yet afforded it. Chapter 6 on covert methods is an amalgam of many methods that merit more consideration than a single chapter can readily provide. Future work will certainly require expanded coverage of this area. Chapter 7 offers brief summaries of each chapter and introduces the reader to some implications of self-control efforts, such as behavioral humanism and the need to teach self-control skills at the school and community level.

In writing this text, we are indebted to a number of environmental influences—family members, colleagues, students, clients, and physical settings. The environmental support of the Stanford Center for Research and Development in Teaching is gratefully acknowledged. The intellectual contribution of Albert Bandura has proved extremely valuable—he has been a very influential model for us. David Rosenhan offered constructive criticism of manuscript drafts which enabled us to present ideas more clearly, concisely, and correctly. Leslie Wolcott demonstrated exceptional talent in taking our vague ideas and creating the illustrations. For her patient and careful editorial help Kathy Nevils merits our appreciation. Ann Gladstone and Sharon Washington provided valuable assistance in typing endless drafts of the manuscript. We were also assisted by the "reality of client experiences." Our efforts to help clients change their actions through self-control techniques continue to teach us a great deal by helping us know that we don't know.

Katherine Thoresen and Fran Mahoney contributed significantly in our efforts to control our own reading, writing, and thinking behavior. In an effort to practice what we preach, we found our own self-control actions very influential. Several procedures were helpful: Self-observing the number of minutes spent writing and posting this data on the office door provided encouragement (and prompts to get busy!) from others. By arranging self-rewarding events (e.g., dinner out in San Francisco) contingent on completing a certain number of pages and by using self-punishment, we were able to maintain our schedule.

In all these efforts, those mentioned above were very instrumental— a concrete example of how self-control (successful and otherwise) is really an environmental endeavor. We appreciate and acknowldge these many environments.

Stanford, Calif.   C. E. T.
University Park, Pa.   M. J. M.

Contents

behavioral
self-control

Chapter

1

Self-Control:
An Introduction

The history of man has been a history of control. Having begun almost entirely at the mercy of his external environment, man has gradually developed a substantial amount of environmental control. Today he has the power to change a wide range of significant environmental events, from irrigating arid farmland to cooling his home in summer. In this quest for survival, however, one area has remained as a persistent challenge to man's capabilities—the area of self-control. For ages men have sought to change and control themselves as they have changed and controlled their external environments. Habit modification, self-improvement, and similar endeavors have been attempted for centuries. Seneca, Pythagoras, Locke,

Goethe, Carlyle, Milton, and Shakespeare, among many others, have lauded the "virtue" of self-control. The literatures of religion, both Eastern and Western, abound with entreaties toward restraint and personal self-fulfillment.

Only recently, however, has the phenomenon labeled "self-control" undergone scientific analysis and controlled application. Just as the early physical sciences made dramatic progress after replacing mystical explanations with more empirical ones, the area of self-control has benefited tremendously from recent attempts to "de-homunculize" it and thereby facilitate scientific analysis. The mystical "little man inside" perspective is being replaced by one that considers self-control as behavior influenced by the environment. A surge of research interest in the area of self-control has ensued—interest in identifying its component processes and in developing effective means for teaching self-control. It is our intent to review and discuss some of the existing evidence and theory about self-control. Before beginning our review, however, the relevance and evolution of self-control patterns merit further attention.

THE RELEVANCE OF SELF–CONTROL

Are there any ethical or pragmatic reasons for one to desire self-control? Actually, there are several possible reasons for the high value placed on a person's ability to control his own actions. For one thing, there is little doubt that many self-control patterns possess survival value of one form or another. A person's ability to control his own body weight, for example, has been shown to have considerable influence on health and longevity (Stuart & Davis, 1972). A second reason for the high status of self-control lies in its relationship to socialization processes. Many contemporary writers have discussed the role of self-regulation in mediating the influence of social mores and customs (Bandura & Walters, 1963; Aronfreed, 1968; Kanfer, 1971). A major goal of training in many cultures is to enable persons to direct, maintain, and coordinate their actions without continuous surveillance. The ability to control one's own actions in the absence of immediate external constraints—to postpone or forego gratifications, to endure avoidable pain, to direct oneself—is typically thought to characterize an intelligent person. Self-control is often considered the ultimate mark of socialization. It is a behavior pattern seen very rarely in infrahumans and sometimes rarely even in humans.

In addition to their social and survival values, self-control behaviors seem marked by a motivation all their own. The contention has been that self-control described in terms of personal freedom, choice, and self-determination is "intrinsically" rewarding.

Freedom, Choice, and
Self-Determination

Some evidence suggests that a person's *perceived* control over his environment can motivate the person to act (Lefcourt, 1966; Rotter, Chance, & Phares, 1972). Since the person is himself a major part of his own environment, the ability to self-control may have some rewarding value. Similar arguments could be extrapolated from the literature showing that exploratory behavior, problem solving, and the ability to manipulate environmental stimulation can encourage action. The question of whether self-regulation is more rewarding than external regulation has, unfortunately, received more speculation than research attention. Recently, for example, Mahoney, Bandura, Dirks, and Wright (1973) completed a study in which monkeys were allowed to choose between self-control and external control of their reinforcements (banana pellets). The data from this experiment revealed that a strong preference for self-control can be demonstrated even in some animals.

Recent research in the area of choice has provided evidence that certain aspects of self-regulation and choice may possess reinforcing properties. In a series of studies (Lovitt, 1969; Lovitt & Curtiss, 1969), children were found to exhibit higher rates of academic behaviors (studying, problem solving) when they were allowed to choose their own reinforcers and the contingencies for earning them. These studies demonstrated that individual response rates were higher even when the currently self-imposed reinforcement conditions were *identical* to those previously or subsequently imposed by a teacher. This, of course, suggests that the ability to choose one's own reward conditions has a significant influence on performance. Corroborative research on the motivational properties of choice is provided by Brigham and his co-workers (Brigham & Bushell, 1972; Brigham & Sherman, in press), who have found that children will work to earn control over their own rewards. In one experiment (Brigham & Bushell, 1972), children could work on one of two tasks for candy rewards. For one task the experimenter chose the reward (i.e., type of candy), while in the second task the child was allowed to choose. Individual data showed that choice was a very strong reinforcer. An intriguing animal experiment by Catania (1972) also supports the notion that choice possesses motivational properties. Pigeons preferred a condition in which they could earn reinforcement on either of two keys over a condition in which only one key was available. Reinforcement schedules were identical in both conditions. Thus choice was the motivating variable. Other researchers (Voss & Homzie, 1970) have reported that rats prefer choice over no-choice options.

Speculations about the intrinsic reward value of personal freedom

are more difficult to evaluate. The term "freedom" is used in at least two different senses. From a philosophical point of view, freedom may imply "free will"—the ability to override or initiate causal patterns of behavior. Although argument on the free will-versus-determinism issue may still be found, most contemporary scientists have adopted a deterministic stance. On the other hand, the lay public and some philosophers continue to support the free-will doctrine. The important point, however, is not whether free will exists. Rather the significant fact from a psychological viewpoint is that most people act *as if* it does. The typical person believes that he possesses free will. This fact is probably far more important than the philosophical issue itself (Kanfer & Karoly, 1972a). As was mentioned earlier, there is some evidence to suggest that this belief may have a very significant impact on an individual's efforts in changing both himself and the environment in which he lives.

A deterministic approach to behavior does not of course imply that the individual can only respond passively to environmental forces. Rather, it simply contends that an individual's responses—even those directed at self-change—are influenced by other events such as socially acquired personal goals and prevailing environmental circumstances. These influences are, in turn, determined by still other factors such as previous learning experiences. The environmental influences to which a person responds are frequently under his control so that he may take an active role in determining his own actions. This interdependent relationship between the person and his environment will be explored further in the next section.

The second meaning of the term "freedom" has to do with the number of alternatives available. Does the person have response options from which to select? Freedom in this sense overlaps with our previous discussion of choice—an individual is free to the extent that he may choose from among several behavioral alternatives. This "behavioral freedom," as contrasted with the philosophical variety, focuses on the diversity of environmental options and the breadth of individual response repertoires. It is interesting to note that, in marked contradiction to arguments that portray behaviorally oriented therapies as "funneling" man's complexity into a few discrete simple categories, these therapies usually emphasize the expansion of behavioral freedom (Thoresen & Hosford, 1973). By increasing the number of responses available to an individual, he is "freed" from previous limitations imposed by such things as learning deficits and fears and anxieties that have led to avoidance responses. Indeed, the availability of a diversity of behavior plays an important role in evolutionary development and even survival (Skinner, 1969).

To summarize, there is some preliminary evidence suggesting that self-control may possess motivating or reinforcing properties. The ability to choose among response options, reinforcement conditions, or types of reward may be reinforcing. Speculation and extrapolation from other fields of research have also pointed up the significance of control over the environment and the value of a diversity of responses. Unfortunately, the paucity of research on these issues precludes any definite conclusions at this time. Our discussion of personal freedom has touched upon another relevant aspect of self-control—namely, its role in the ongoing controversy between behavioristic and humanistic psychologists.

Behavioral Humanism and Self-Control

One area that has generated considerable controversy during the last twenty years has to do with the relationship between "behavioristic" and "humanistic" approaches to psychology and education. The former has traditionally been characterized as rigidly empirical and preoccupied with readily observable behaviors. The latter might be described as loosely empirical with an emphasis on cognitive, emotional, and similar, essentially covert phenomena. For many years the controversy has raged as to which of these approaches is "better," i.e., more productive, cogent, or effective. Behaviorists have criticized humanistic psychologists for their "soft-minded" approach. The latter have voiced frequent rebuttals centering on the myopia of a viewpoint which ignores or de-emphasizes the role of private events in human behavior. The persistence of this controversy is exemplified by this recent quotation from Floyd W. Matson (1971):

> Plainly, the differences between us must be very deep—not just technical or strategic or methodological but philosophical, and perhaps moral. For my part, I believe that Skinner and his gentle friends state the case against their own philosophy so openly and candidly that one need only cry "Hark! See there? They are exposing themselves (the Grand Conditioner has no clothes)!" On the other hand, the Skinnerians perceive themselves not only as warmly clothed but gorgeously arrayed: Wrapped in the mantle of Science, armed with the tools of the "technology of behavior," they walk the green pastures of Walden Two and marvel at their adversaries, who speak a gibberish compounded of nonsense syllables such as "freedom," "person," "choice," "responsibility," "mind," and so on (p. 2).

Thus the issue is still a hotly debated one. However, recent developments in the areas of self-control and "cognitive behaviorism" have addressed themselves to some of the major issues in the behaviorism–humanism debate. Controlled empirical inquiries into significant private events (thoughts, images, feelings) have begun to appear in the literature. These studies, while they may not eliminate further debate, point in the direction of a "behavioral humanism"—that is, a scientific approach to human behavior that neither ignores nor de-emphasizes cognitive phenomena (Thoresen, 1973a). Such an approach is particularly germane to the area of self-control. In order to explore the processes and parameters of self-control phenomena, an *empirical* viewpoint is essential. Such a viewpoint must, however, allow the study of *all* relevant behaviors—both overt and covert—that have a bearing on self-control. This means that a scientific study of self-control may sometimes necessitate partial reliance on self-reported unobservable phenomena (cf. Mahoney, 1970). To the extent that internal events aid in clarifying our understanding of behavior, their inclusion in a science of behavior is both justified and advisable (Skinner, 1963).

The area of self-control provides some unique possibilities for a rapprochement of the behavioristic and humanistic viewpoints. By translating humanistic goals and concerns into behavioral objectives, principles of behavior change may be drawn upon to facilitate humanistic ends (Thoresen, 1973a). Since many of these goals involve private, intrapersonal phenomena (thoughts, feelings, images) that are accessible only to the person, their attainment must necessarily involve some degree of self-awareness and self-regulation. Similarly, the high esteem in which freedom and choice are held by humanistic psychologists suggests a promising relationship with self-control approaches. Perhaps as the polemics between behaviorists and humanists subside, a more productive and effective improvement of the human situation will ensue (Houts & Serber, 1972). Behavioral self-control offers the technology for effecting such improvements.

The Pragmatics of Self-Control

One final area bearing on the relevance of self-control has to do with practical value. The presumed advantages and disadvantages of self-regulatory strategies have been touched upon elsewhere (e.g., Cautela, 1969a; Kopel, 1972). On the positive side, the inexpensiveness and portability of self-control can be pointed to. If a person can be helped to manage his own behavior, less professional time may be required for the desired behavior change. Moreover, the person may be the best possible agent to change his own behavior—he certainly has much more frequent access to it than anyone else, particularly when the behavior is covert. Self-control strategies may also avoid some of the generalization and maintenance problems that often plague therapist-centered strategies. There is evidence supporting the clinical importance of using naturalistic (real-life) situations as the training grounds for therapeutic behavior change (e.g., Patterson, 1973). Such efforts enable the individual to develop appropriate skills in the very situation in which they will be applied. Problems of transfer from laboratory or consulting room to real-life problems are thereby avoided. Since self-control techniques can be implemented in naturalistic situations, they facilitate this transfer. Finally, training in self-control may provide an individual with technical and analytic talents that will facilitate subsequent attempts at self-control with different behaviors. These pragmatic advantages of self-control merit serious consideration and evaluation by clinicians and researchers (Jeffrey, 1974).

CONCEPTS OF SELF–CONTROL

The area of self-control has long been beset by a host of terminological confusions and misconceptions. For example, the term "self-control" is often interpreted as being synonymous with "restraint," so that only actions that inhibit responses qualify. Moreover, the labels of "self-regulation," "self-control," and "self-management" are often used differently by researchers. By far the most significant conceptual issue, however, is that which deals with the definition of self-control. There are two basic viewpoints on this issue: (1) traditional "willpower" conceptions, and (2) functional "behavioral" conceptions.

Traditional Views: Willpower

The most prevalent conception of self-control has been one that emphasizes the role of "willpower." Willpower is, in turn, defined as a personality trait or psychic force that enables the person to exhibit control over his own actions. The inadequacies of the willpower approach are numerous. First of all, the concept of willpower suffers from logical circularity. In one's attempt to explain some behavior by reference to an internal psychic force, the referent for the latter is the very behavior it is supposed to explain. For example, suppose that Mary has lost 25 pounds by rigidly adhering to a diet of prunes for one month. Her friends attribute her steadfast dieting to her willpower and intestinal fortitude (the latter is a *must* on prune diets). How do they know she possesses "willpower"? Well, she has stuck to an unsavory diet, hasn't she? The point is that a behavior (steadfast dieting) is used to ascertain the presence of an internal state (willpower) that is in turn used to explain the original behavior (steadfast dieting). This circularity poses the threat of disguising a double description as an explanation.

In addition to their circularity, willpower conceptions suffer from many of the problems that plague "mentalistic" approaches to behavior (cf. Skinner, 1953, 1963, 1969). For example, they tend to discourage the continuation or expansion of partially successful self-control attempts. If an individual attributes the failure of his first attempt to quit smoking to a lack of willpower, he will be much less inclined to pursue actively new attempts to improve his self-controlling capabilities. A person who perceives himself as lacking willpower typically views his vices or deficiencies in a fatalistic "I can't help it . . . what's the use" fashion. Such an attitude, whereby the person attributes his actions to forces beyond his control, clearly discourages efforts at self-control. Related to this helpless attitude is the tendency to view willpower and self-control as a simple dichotomy—you've either got it (willpower) or you don't.

The inadequacies of the willpower approach to self-control do not stem from their inherently mentalistic nature. The viability of a concept is determined by its utility in predicting and explaining functional relationships. Thus an intrapsychic conception of self-control is acceptable so long as it demonstrates its utility. However, as is true of many trait-oriented approaches to behavior (cf. Mischel, 1968, 1971, in press), willpower has not yet shown itself to be a helpful concept in the experimental analysis of self-control.

Behavioral Views: Functional Relations

Research over the past decade has indicated that a person's ability to control his own actions is very much a function of his knowledge and control of current situational factors. That is, self-control skills are tightly

bound up with the person's ability to discriminate patterns and causes in the behaviors to be regulated—e.g., cues or events that frequently precede overeating or certain consequences that often follow smoking. In essence, the old Greek maxim "know thyself" can be paraphrased to "know thy controlling variables."

To exercise self-control the individual must understand what factors influence his actions and how he can alter those factors to bring about the changes he desires. This understanding requires that the individual in effect become a sort of personal scientist (Kelly, 1955). The person begins by observing what goes on, recording and analyzing personal "data," using certain techniques to change specific things (e.g., thought patterns or the physical environment), and, finally, deciding if the desired change has occurred. Again, in making such a decision, the person looks to the data about himself.

The behavioral approach to self-control is one that emphasizes the relationship between a person's behaviors and his environment. This does not mean that such things as "motivation" and past history are de-emphasized. On the contrary, these variables play an important role in a behavioral conception. Likewise, the term "behavior" is defined very broadly

—thoughts, feelings, and images are just as "behavioral" as push-ups and conversation.

The functional relationship between behavior and environment was formulated by Goldiamond (1965a) in the equation $B=f(x)$. A person's behavior (B) is a function (f) of his environment (x). That is, by arranging specific environmental conditions, one can predictably control the occurrence (or nonoccurrence) of a specific behavior. The arrangement of these environmental conditions can be performed by some external agent (therapist, parent, teacher) *or* by the person himself. In the case of the latter, a new and even more significant equation for self-control results: $x=f(B)$. An individual's environment (x) is a function (f) of his behavior (B). This *interdependence* of behavior and environment is one that cannot be overemphasized in self-regulation (Bandura, 1971b). The self-controlling individual must engage in certain behaviors that alter his environment in ways that systematically modify other relevant behaviors. In this way the person influences the situations of his life and, in turn, is influenced by them.

When viewing self-control from a behavioral perspective, an important distinction is that between "controlled" and "controlling" responses (Skinner, 1953). The controlled response is behavior to be changed (B in Goldiamond's equation). This change is brought about by altering environmental variables (e.g., response consequences or environmental cues). The act of manipulating those environmental variables is the "controlling response" B in equation $x=f(B)$. The controlled–controlling distinction is an extremely important one. If one assumes that behaviors may be modified by their consequences, then this applies not only to the controlled behavior in the above formulation but also to the *controlling* behaviors. Self-controlling behaviors, *like any other* action, must be appropriately rewarded if they are to be maintained.

The behavioral approach to self-control contains certain subemphases that differentiate various workers in the field. One contemporary issue concerns the role of individual versus situational variables in self-control phenomena. Stuart (1972), for example, believes that the concept of self-control suffers from many of the conceptual problems characteristic of traditional willpower approaches. He argues for situational control of behavior—that is, the arrangement of environmental variables in such a way that behavior change is produced. However, the act of arranging one's environment in order to facilitate behavior change is itself a demonstration of self-control. Although self-control researchers are well advised to beware of conceptual confusions, we contend that a behavioral view of *self*-control is viable on pragmatic and empirical grounds. A wealth of evidence shows that situational variables do modify behavior, but it is the person's own manipulation of those variables that requires the concept of self-control.

CRITERIA FOR SELF–CONTROL

In order to evaluate the processes and parameters of "self-control," one must first specify exactly what is meant by that term. Conventional definitions usually equate self-control with "restraint"—the ability to inhibit a response in the face of temptation. However, what about the individual who undertakes a daily routine of strenuous exercise or the person who writes himself notes as cues for daily tasks? Is the reformed smoker, abstinent for five years, still exhibiting self-control when he turns down a cigarette? One of the crucial features in any definition of self-control is the term "self." What is it that differentiates self-control from external control?

Continuum or Category

The cardinal feature of self-control is that it is the person himself who is the agent of his own behavior change.[1] The role of the person in this change has been a long-standing issue. Skinner (1953), among others, has maintained that all instances of self-control are ultimately maintained by external variables.[2] For example, a person who employs various self-control techniques in order to quit smoking may actually be under the ultimate control of such external variables as health considerations, family requests, or financial matters. Recalling the controlled–controlling distinction, Skinner's contention is that the response of controlling one's own behavior is usually externally reinforced (by such things as social praise and financial or physical rewards). The reciprocal interaction between self-control and external control systems is important to keep in mind.

The classification of a particular instance is seldom so clear-cut that one can immediately label it self-control or external control. The complexity of interacting variables in self-control situations is often overwhelming.

---

[1] The above conceptualization should not be interpreted as suggesting "soft determinism"—whereby the individual overrides a causal determinism by generating some "self-willed" cause. Although the individual is the "agent" of change in self-control, his act of engaging in (or not engaging in) self-regulatory responses is just as much determined by causal forces as any other act. This does not make his act less self-regulatory in nature, just as the fact that a choice has been caused does not make it any less of a choice (Kaplan, 1964).

[2] The term "external" is used here in two different senses. When used in reference to the location of environmental variables, external denotes stimuli outside of the person's skin. Since there is now considerable evidence questioning the utility of dichotomizing behaviors and/or cues on the basis of their relation to one's skin, the internal–external distinction here is simply a descriptive one. When the term "external" is used in reference to locus of control, it denotes a situation or variable that is not under the immediate or direct control of the person.

A *continuum* classification is, therefore, more appropriate. A behavior pattern may be compared to other behavior patterns with regard to the relative frequency, form, timing, and magnitude of external versus self-control components. External variables are those over which the person has no immediate or direct control. Hence it makes sense to speak of various degrees of self-control. For example, a person who devises and executes his own self-control regimen might be classified as exhibiting more self-control than one who was tutored and then weaned of external support. We must be careful, however, not to succumb to the fallacy of assuming that increasing degrees of self-control are somehow "better" or more effective. Such a relationship remains to be demonstrated.

Self-Control Criteria

One of the difficulties in arriving at an objective and explicit definition of self-control has to do with its social relativity. Levine (1973) points out that the designation of a particular pattern of behavior as "self-control" is very much a social labeling process. There are no qualitative differences between "self-control" and "non-self-control" behaviors. Rather, the differences lie in their social context, the conspicuousness of external influences, and the perspective of the labeler. In this sense the social relativity of other psychological terms, such as "abnormality," "mental illness," and "personality," is shared by concepts of self-control. For example, the behavior pattern of self-imposed starvation is labeled differently depending on whether the person is an obese housewife, a prison inmate, or an anorexic. The social desirability of the controlled response also enters into most common definitions. Undesirable behavior patterns are seldom accorded the label of self-control. Levine (1973) points out that the assumption of "effort" is usually connoted in self-regulatory labels. A performance must involve some amount of conscious effort before most people will label it self-control.

Table 1–1 illustrates the rich variety of behaviors that have been designated as self-regulatory. In an attempt to synthesize some of the common features found in these various forms of self-control, the following tentative definition is proposed: *A person displays self-control when in the relative absence of immediate external constraints, he engages in behavior whose previous probability has been less than that of alternatively available behaviors* (involving lesser or delayed reward, greater exertion or aversive properties, and so on). This response pattern is often influenced by delayed environmental consequences (e.g., social praise, health improvement, material aggrandizement, etc.). The designation of a behavior pattern as self-regulatory is a socially relative labeling process.

The above definition, which draws heavily upon Premack's work

TABLE 1–1 FORMS OF SELF-CONTROL

Skinner (1953):
1. Physical restraint and physical aid
2. Stimulus manipulation (including self-managed stimulus exposure)
3. Deprivation and satiation
4. Manipulation of emotional conditions (controlling predispositions, rehearsal of previous consequences, self-instruction)
5. Aversive stimulation
6. Drugs (anesthetics, aphrodisiacs)
7. Operant conditioning (self-reinforcement and self-managed extinction)
8. Punishment
9. Incompatible response approach ("doing something else")
10. Private events (cognitive consequation)

Bandura and Walters (1963):
1. Resistance to deviation
2. Regulation of self-administered rewarding resources
3. Delay of gratification

Ferster (1965):
1. Alteration of behavior-environment relations to reduce ultimately aversive consequences
2. Performances which increase long-range effectiveness (e.g., music lessons)
3. Alteration of the physical environment (rather than individual's behavior)

Goldiamond (1965a):
1. Alteration of specified environmental variables that control one's behavior
2. Application of functional behavior analysis

Cautela (1969a):
1. Reciprocal inhibition techniques (relaxation, desensitization, thought stopping, covert sensitization, assertive training)
2. Operant procedures

Kanfer (1970a):
1. Abstention despite ad lib availability of reinforcers
2. Execution of a behavior despite its known aversive consequences

Stuart (1970):
1. Aversive procedures
2. Instigation techniques

Kanfer (1971):
1. Competing responses approach
2. Manipulation of aversive consequences
3. Manipulation of target behaviors' consequences (includes reduction and delay of positive consequences, negative consequation for antecedent responses, and differential reinforcement of other behaviors)
4. Environment manipulation
5. Self-reward

(1965, 1971) in reinforcement theory, simply states that a "self-controlling" person engages in responses that have been relatively unlikely in previous situations. Thus the individual who has usually smoked at parties is exhibiting self-control if—in the absence of externally controlled factors such as physical illness or the unavailability of cigarettes—he refrains from smoking at a party. Note that as the individual becomes more successful in his self-control patterns, the previous probability of the response to be controlled diminishes so that a relatively lesser degree of self-control is exhibited.

As with most definitions in behavioral science, the above may be less than perfect in terms of technical interpretation. However, as a tentative description of what is meant by self-control, the foregoing may prove useful in the exploration and understanding of available evidence. The definition points up three important features of classical self-control phenomena—(1) they always involve two or more alternative behaviors, (2) the consequences of those behaviors are usually conflicting, and (3) the self-regulatory pattern is usually prompted and/or maintained by external factors such as long-term consequences. For example, the individual who chooses to quit smoking has the option to (1) smoke or (2) not to smoke. Or he may do such things as chew gum or suck on candy. The consequences of smoking are immediately pleasant but ultimately aversive while the consequences of not smoking are just the opposite. Moreover, the person's attempt to regulate his smoking behavior does not take place in an environmental vacuum—he is affected by such things as doctor's orders, remarks by family or friends, health changes, and so on.

The "immediate anti-hedonism" or conflicting consequences (Kanfer, 1970a) feature of the above definition does not belie a contradiction of the reinforcement principle. Some (e.g., Gewirtz, 1971) who have criticized self-control conceptualizations because of their alleged incompatibility with learning theory have apparently overlooked the abundance of evidence indicating that—just like other behavior patterns—self-controlling responses are a function of their consequences. Viewing the self-control sequence at a molar level, the definition simply states that, given ultimate and sufficient incentives, a person will display response patterns whose immediate consequences may appear nonreinforcing.

The temporal gradient of consequences is a key factor in the definition and conceptualization of self-regulation. Generally speaking, a self-control attempt always involves the acceleration (increase) or deceleration (decrease) of one or more responses. In accelerative self-control, the pretreatment gradient is usually one where the immediate consequences of a behavior are aversive but its delayed consequences are pleasant (e.g., physical exercise). On the other hand, responses which become the target for decelerative self-control usually have pleasant immediate effects but aversive delayed consequences (e.g., overeating, alcoholism). Self-control strategies often attempt to "bridge" the gradient of consequences by reversing or reducing the contrast. For example, the delayed aversive effects of smoking may be made more immediate or its immediate pleasant consequences may be reduced.

Since many self-control efforts have very delayed consequences, the role of mediating factors should not be overlooked. Researchers who avoid symbolic processes in their efforts to explain self-control patterns face an insurmountable task. As Bandura (1969) has pointed out, most instances of human behavior result not only in environmental consequences but also in self-evaluative reactions. Individuals mediate and modify environmental influences through such socially learned behaviors as goal-setting, evaluative comparisons, self-approval, and self-criticism. Thus, while the radical behaviorist may be perplexed by the tenacity of self-controlling responses in the absence of observable environmental influences, the researcher familiar with social learning processes recognizes the significant mediating role of self-reactions in maintaining certain behaviors.

Behavior patterns conforming to the above definition are called self-control, self-regulation, and/or self-management. As an aid to conceptualization, a tentative systems model of self-control is presented. That model, seen in Figure 1–1, approaches self-control in a component processes manner. Each element or process found in the model is also found in most instances of self-control. Note that the model is dynamic and should not be read as a chronological flow chart. The antecedent or

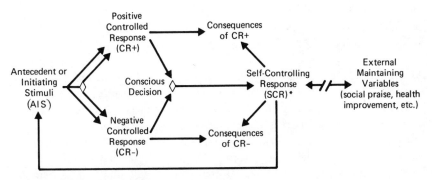

*Self-Controlling Responses (SCRs):

1. Environmental Planning

    a) AIS modification (stimulus control) and preprogramming of CR consequences
    b) Self-regulated stimulus exposure (e.g., self-administered desensitization)
    c) Self-instructions

2. Behavioral Programming

    a) Self-observation
    b) Self-reward (positive and negative, overt and covert)
    c) Self-punishment (positive and negative, overt and covert)

Figure 1–1   A systems model of self-control.

initiating stimuli (AIS) are those cues that precede the controlled response (CR+ or CR—). In the case of overeating, hunger pangs or a candy machine may be the AIS. The positive controlled response (CR+) is that behavior whose likelihood is to be increased (e.g., *not* eating fattening foods). The negative controlled behavior (CR—) is the behavior that is to be decelerated (e.g., overeating). In long-standing habit patterns, the AIS may be either nonexistent or unspecified. For example, Premack (1971) has discussed the nearly automatic sequence wherein habitual smokers light up a cigarette without any awareness either of the act itself or of any antecedent cues. When the AIS-CR relationship is more explicit, a conscious decision may be involved (represented by a triangle in Figure 1–1). Evaluative features may enter into this response choice and may also be present following the occurrence of a CR.

The probability of a CR may be modified by various self-controlling responses (SCRs). This is usually done either by altering the consequences of one or more CRs or by change of the AIS. For example, an individual might regulate his spending behavior either by rewarding himself for frugality (CR+), by punishing himself for inordinate spending (CR—), or by avoiding those shops where his spending behavior is a problem (AIS). Evaluative features may be involved in SCR. As will be seen in a later chapter, the simple recording of responses to be controlled (self-observation) will often alter the probability of those responses. Self-controlling responses (SCRs) are modified and maintained by their effectiveness in altering CRs as well as by a variety of external factors.

GENERAL SELF–CONTROL STRATEGIES

As mentioned earlier and illustrated in Figure 1–1, there are two basic forms of SCRs. The first involves *environmental planning*, wherein the individual plans and implements changes in relevant situational factors *prior* to the execution of a target behavior. For example, the reformed smoker might leave the house in the morning without sufficient change to buy cigarettes. He might also inform all of his friends that he is trying to kick the habit and would appreciate their criticism if they see him smoking. Both of these strategies involve a prechange of environmental variables. Discarding any cigarettes that had been stored in one's house would also entail AIS modification. In general, self-control is exhibited in environmental strategies prior to the execution of a CR, as when an individual places a gentle reminder on his favorite box of sweets or asks his wife to scold him for overeating.

The second general strategy, called *behavioral programming*, involves self-administered consequences *following* the occurrence of a target response. Rewarding oneself with a special purchase after completing a task illustrates this strategy. While environmental self-control strategies are usually implemented prior to the to-be-controlled response, behavioral programming strategies come into play after the response has already occurred. Examples would include a student's self-criticism after failing an exam, the housewife's self-recording of her grocery spending, and the golfer's self-praise after a 30-foot putt. The self-presented consequences may be verbal, imaginal, or material.

The above distinction between environmental planning and behavioral programming strategies is, of course, an arbitrary one. There are many instances in which their differentiation is neither simple nor useful. Most clinical applications of self-control involve complex combinations of the two strategies. For purposes of clarification, however, we shall discuss them separately. It should be remembered that the principles governing the effects of the two strategies are presumed to be uniform. Their differentiation is based on relative emphasis: *Behavioral programming* strategies highlight the consequences of a *behavior*, while *environmental planning* strategies emphasize various features of the person's *environment*.

Environmental Planning
(Stimulus Control)

Some of the earliest work in self-regulation dealt with the alteration of stimuli that influence the occurrence of target behaviors. For this reason, what we have labeled environmental planning strategies are also frequently referred to as stimulus-control procedures. Essentially, these strategies involve the association of undesired responses (CR—s) with stimuli that are gradually reduced in frequency. Simultaneously, desired responses (CR+s) are linked to stimuli whose frequency is systematically increased. This rationale was derived from laboratory research demonstrating that the probability of a response is dramatically influenced by the presence or absence of stimulus cues previously associated with that response.

Self-regulation based on stimulus-control techniques was first introduced by Ferster, Nurnberger, and Levitt (1962), who outlined their feasibility for self-managed weight control. These researchers pointed out that eating responses are frequently associated with many environmental cues that subsequently gain control over the responses and repeatedly set the occasion for their occurrence. For example, the average person eats not only at the dinner table, but while watching television, studying, reading, and working. Because these myriad cues have been associated with eating in the past, the individual may inadvertently engage in eating whenever he encounters them. The kitchen and overstuffed chair become frequent elicitors of eating, as do restaurants, vending machines, and food displays. Ferster and his colleagues suggested that an effective means of controlling overeating would be to decrease selectively the number of environmental cues associated with eating. They recommended that individuals restrict their eating to a few relatively infrequent situations and that they engage in no other distracting or rewarding activities (e.g., reading, television viewing) while eating. Emphasis was also placed on the "ultimate aversive consequences" of overeating and on the development of incompatible behaviors to eating.

These techniques were implemented and expanded by Stuart (1967), who successfully treated eight obese women. The magnitude of weight loss reported by those subjects over a twelve-month period ranged from 26 to 47 pounds and represented one of the most successful obesity studies ever reported. The very impressive results of this first application have since been repeatedly replicated (Harris, 1969; Hagen, 1970; Wollersheim, 1970; Penick, Filion, Fox, & Stunkard, 1971; Stuart, 1971; Jeffrey, Christensen, & Pappas, 1972). Excellent reviews of the existing evidence on stimulus-control strategies in obesity are provided by Stunkard (1972) and Stuart and Davis (1972). In previewing our discussion of those self-control techniques labeled behavioral programming strategies, it should be pointed out that many of the above studies combined the two basic approaches, environmental planning and behavioral programming. Indeed, there is some evidence that their combination may be a necessary factor in the successful treatment of some problem behaviors (Mahoney, Moura, & Wade, 1973).

The application of environmental planning strategies to other self-control problems has likewise met with considerable success. Fox (1962) presented an excellent outline for the implementation of stimulus-control procedures as a means for developing appropriate study skills. The fundamental strategy was to design an environment conducive to studying and to establish direct associations between specific stimuli and study behavior. For one student this meant that studying—and *only* studying—was to be performed in one room. If behaviors incompatible with studying occurred (daydreaming, for example) the student was instructed to leave the room immediately. This prevented an inadvertent association of inappropriate responses with the study room. Other strategies included the use of small, but gradually increasing study assignments ("shaping"), reinforcement, and a structured format for studying (the SQ3R technique). Results from a pilot study with five students were very impressive. All five increased their quarter grade-point average by at least one letter grade. One subject went from an F average to a B average in two quarters.

This early pilot work by Fox was extended and replicated by Beneke and Harris (1972). Despite a high attrition (dropout) rate and the use of early dropouts as control subjects, Beneke and Harris were able to report significant increases in grade-point average among students who were taught stimulus control, shaping, reinforcement, and SQ3R review methods.

Several case studies have also found stimulus-control procedures to be very effective in the treatment of a wide range of behavior problems. Goldiamond (1965a), for example, reported their success with clients exhibiting marital discord, obesity, poor study habits, and sulking. In one case, a couple's bedroom bickering and lack of lovemaking was modified by introducing a novel bedroom stimulus (a yellow night light), which signified "make love, not war." Bergin (1969) used variations of a stimulus-control theme in the successful treatment of sexual deviation. Two homosexual clients were taught to interrupt and divert deviant behavior patterns by altering their controlling stimuli.

Another behavior that has been frequently treated with stimulus-control procedures is smoking. The rationale here, of course, is that smoking often becomes associated with a wide range of frequently occur-ring environmental cues (e.g., completion of a meal, smelling or observing another individual's smoking, or sight of an ashtray). Nolan (1968) and Roberts (1969) reported success in their treatment of excessive smoking by using the rather straightforward technique of restricting that behavior to a special "smoking chair," which was conveniently placed in nonenter-taining surroundings. In order to smoke, the individual had to retire to

this chair (located, for example, in the garage), have his cigarette alone, and then return to the house. An interesting anecdote regarding possible pitfalls in this strategy was recently reported to the authors. A therapist who wanted to reduce his own cigarette consumption decided to establish stimulus control by restricting his smoking to the bathroom at home and at work. Shortly after initiating this strategy, he found that the sight or smell of other people's cigarettes made him want to urinate!

More systematic studies on the application of environmental planning strategies to smoking have been reported by Upper and Meredith (1970, 1971) and by others (e.g., Levinson, Shapiro, Schwartz, & Tursky, 1971; Shapiro, Tursky, Schwartz, & Shnidman, 1971; Bernard & Efran, 1972). In these inquiries, smoking was reduced by having persons associate smoking with a novel environmental stimulus. Smokers were asked to carry small portable parking-meter timers and to allow themselves a cigarette only when given an audible cue from their timer. The timers were initially set to go off after intervals that were equal to the smoker's average period between cigarettes. This meant that persons began breaking previous associations between smoking and everyday cues, such as a cup of coffee or the end of a meal. They simultaneously set up new and novel stimuli that were under the smoker's control and that became the sole cues for smoking. Subjects were instructed to gradually increase the timer intervals so that the periods between cigarettes were systematically increased. In this manner, their daily smoking frequencies were gradually reduced. Although long-term follow-up data suggested that the improvement brought about by these techniques may have gone the way of countless other smoking reduction efforts (Bernstein, 1969), these studies illustrate the naturalistic application of self-administered stimulus-control strategies.

Another form of environmental planning involves the prearrangement of behavioral consequences. Although this procedure places less emphasis on actual alteration of environmental stimuli, it shares the characteristic of modification or elimination of certain tempting situations before the problem behavior occurs. This technique is sometimes referred to as contingency contracting since it frequently involves a social agreement (contract) regarding the requirements (contingencies) for reward or punishment. Examples of prearranged consequences are numerous. Elliott and Tighe (1968) asked individuals to deposit money with an experimenter, who then rewarded or fined them for their self-regulatory performances. Similarly, Powell and Azrin (1968) devised a special cigarette case that automatically delivered painful electric shock whenever the individual opened it. In an interesting attempt to eliminate smoking, Neisworth (1972) prearranged social reinforcement for progress in gradually delimiting allowable smoking situations. Total abstinence had been maintained at a four-year follow-up. Boudin (1972) reported the successful treatment of excessive amphetamine use by means of contingency contracting. Although other therapeutic strategies were incorporated, the client's contract is noteworthy. The client, a black female, made legally binding arrangements to contribute $50 to the Ku Klux Klan for every violation (use of drugs) of her contract. This prearrangement of financial consequences aided in the successful elimination of amphetamine use. A somewhat similar strategy was used by Mann (1972) in the treatment of obesity. Overweight subjects deposited personal valuables (an extensive record collection, for example) with an experimenter, who then returned or kept them, depending on each subject's weight-loss progress. The therapeutic promise of contingency contracts is supported by several other studies (e.g., Stuart, 1971; Miller, 1972; Kanfer, Cox, Greiner, & Karoly, 1972).

Strategies wherein tempting environmental cues are eliminated or altered (e.g., not buying cigarettes, replacing fattening refrigerator contents with dietetic substitutes, and so forth) are likewise instances of environmental planning. Self-instructions, for example, are a very effective means of directing and initiating behavior (Bem, 1967; O'Leary, 1968). In a series of studies, Meichenbaum and his colleagues (Meichenbaum, Gilmore, & Fedoravicius, 1971; Meichenbaum & Goodman, 1971; Meichenbaum & Cameron, 1974) have demonstrated the importance of "internal" stimulus control in adaptive behavior change. With subjects ranging from speech-anxious college students to institutionalized schizophrenics, these researchers have reported dramatically impressive successes. Their techniques involve progressive internalization of instructional cues, such that the individual averts maladaptive internal monologues (e.g., "I know I'm going to flunk this test") and substitutes relevant coping cues (e.g., "You're doing fine"). These promising techniques will be discussed at length in Chapter 6.

Behavioral Programming
(Self-Presented Consequences)

Self-administered consequences represent a change in one's environment that *follows* rather than precedes the behavior to be controlled. As mentioned earlier, cognitive self-evaluative activities often occur immediately after behaviors. For example, the dieter or reformed smoker engages in numerous instances of positive and negative self-evaluation (self-praise, self-criticism) during his efforts at self-control. These symbolic activities play a crucial role in the maintenance of self-control behaviors. The individual may additionally present himself with tangible consequences after controlled responses. A partial list of behavioral programming SCRs is presented below.

1. *Self-observation*: the recording, charting, and/or display of information relevant to a controlled response (e.g., charting one's weight)

2. *Positive self-reward*: the self-administration or consumption of a freely available reinforcer only after performance of a specific, positive response (e.g., treating one's self to a special event for having lost weight)

3. *Negative self-reward*: the avoidance of or escape from a freely avoidable aversive stimulus only after performance of a specific, positive response (e.g., removing an uncomplimentary pig poster from one's dining room whenever a diet is adhered to for a full day)

4. *Positive self-punishment*: the removal of a freely available reinforcer after the performance of a specific, negative response (e.g., tearing up a dollar bill for every 100 calories in excess of one's daily limit)

5. *Negative self-punishment*: the presentation of a freely avoidable aversive stimulus after the performance of a specific, negative response (e.g., presenting oneself with a noxious odor after each occurrence of snacking)

Note that behavioral programming strategies involve self-imposed contingencies—i.e., the individual presents himself with certain consequences *only* after having exhibited some performance.

The research on self-presented consequences has indicated that these strategies can be very effective in the self-modification of behavior. Substantially more research has been devoted to the investigation of behavioral programming strategies than to environmental planning approaches. The remainder of this book will address itself primarily to an analysis of the effects of self-presented consequences in behavior change. As mentioned earlier, many of the studies reviewed actually represent combinations of the two general SCR strategies outlined in this chapter.

SUMMARY

Self-control is exhibited when a person engages in a behavior whose previous probability has been less than that of alternatively available responses. The response to be controlled in self-management often involves immediately unpleasant but ultimately desired consequences, whereas competing responses involve immediately pleasant but ultimately aversive results. Self-control patterns are usually mediated by symbolic processes and ultimately maintained by external variables. Two basic self-controlling strategies are: (1) environmental planning, whereby the person prearranges relevant environmental cues to influence the occurrence of a behavior, and (2) behavioral programming, whereby the person presents himself with consequences following the occurrence of a target behavior.

Chapter

2

Methodological
Issues in
Self-Control

The investigation and description of principles governing self-control phenomena require, of course, that those phenomena be open to scientific inquiry. If definitive statements are to be made about the processes and parameters of self-control, sound empirical evidence must be available.

The eligibility criteria for scientific inquiry have been previously outlined by philosophers of science and behavioral researchers (cf. Nagel, 1961; Kaplan, 1964; Helmstadter, 1970). In general, one may condense those criteria as follows: To be scientifically respectable, an interest area must generate statements, questions, or hypotheses that are *publicly specifiable* and *testable*. Moreover, evidence brought to bear on a particular issue should be *replicable* by independent researchers.

The public specifiability criterion requires that the hypothesis in question be capable of being presented in a form that can be comprehended by an intelligent public. In other words, if a question or hypothesis cannot be communicated to more than one person, it cannot be scientifically evaluated. There are, of course, many ways to communicate. Sometimes, for example, the phenomenon in question is complex in a way that requires use of analogs to communicate it to others (e.g., a visual or graphic representation of the behavior that cannot be described in numbers [cf. Spence, 1973]). This criterion of specifiability is also brought to bear on the techniques used in investigating a phenomenon. A researcher must be capable of specifying what he did in evaluating some hypothesis. This requirement insures that other interested researchers will be able to replicate the techniques or evaluation in question (cf. Turner, 1967).

The testability criterion requires that the hypothesis in question be capable of being confirmed and/or disconfirmed by evidence. The scientific researcher must be capable of specifying exactly what evidence would be needed to either refute or support the hypothesis. The rationale, limitations, and viability of the testability criterion are discussed at length by Turner (1967).

The replicability criterion stems in part from the inductive nature of many scientific enterprises. If independent researchers perform a similar experiment and get similar results, confidence is gained in their evidence and in the preliminary relationship under study. In other words, if a procedure is repeated several times and similar results are found, one feels more confident that the results were caused by the procedure rather than by some unsuspected variable.

Thus self-control phenomena should be (1) specifiable, (2) testable, and (3) replicable if they are to be considered eligible for empirical evaluation. In Chapter 1 "self-control" was defined as a behavior pattern in which a person freely (i.e., without external coercion) engages in a response whose previous probability has been less than that of alternatively available responses. Moreover, it was stipulated that, in self-control, the emitted response has immediate consequences that are relatively less pleasant than those of other available responses. The remainder of this chapter will be devoted to a discussion of four different methodological issues bearing on the scientific evaluation of self-control patterns. (It will be assumed that the reader has some familiarity with experimental design and research methodology.) Several excellent sources for these areas are Sidman (1960), Campbell and Stanley (1966), Chassan (1967), Helmstadter (1970), and Thoresen (in press). Additional methodological issues in self-management are discussed by Jeffrey (1974).

THE MATTER OF
EXTERNAL CONTROL

A frequently encountered problem in self-control research has to do with the locus of behavior control. When the immediate variables controlling an individual's behavior are in the hands of the individual (i.e., freely manipulable by him), then "internal" or self-control is displayed. However, when immediate controlling variables are beyond the manipulation of the individual, then "external" control is exhibited. A substantial body of evidence now exists indicating that the locus of behavior control (either real or perceived) can have dramatic effects on the behavior in question. This issue will be discussed at greater length in Chapter 7. (A review of some of the research on locus of control is provided by Lefcourt, 1966; Throop & MacDonald, 1971; and Rotter, Chance, & Phares, 1972.)

As pointed out in Chapter 1, it is essential that a behavioral strategy be in the hands of the individual who is allegedly exhibiting self-control. Skinner (1953) has contended that all instances of self-control (and its concomitant strategies) are ultimately instances of external control. One might add that "no behavior is an island alone unto itself." This ongoing reciprocity between internal and external control systems has already been emphasized.

In terms of locus of control, the conditions immediately preceding and/or following some targeted response determine whether it is the person or someone else who is controlling the behavior. When external factors are frequent, large, or temporally immediate, then little room is left for a self-control classification. Recall, however, that our categorization of any particular instance should be done with a continuum (and not a dichotomy) in mind. As a classic example of external control, we might discuss the proverbial rat in the Skinner box. The rat does not exhibit self-control if his access to certain stimuli (food pellets or water, for example) is externally controlled (either by a preprogrammed apparatus, another organism, or chance). In an operant conditioning paradigm, an organism would have to have free access to the crucial stimuli before any behavioral performances could be labeled "self-control." Generally speaking, if some act is required to produce a reinforcement or to avoid or escape from a punishment, then some degree of external control is involved. However, if an organism has free access to reinforcers and yet repeatedly displays effortful performances prior to their consumption, then self-control is exhibited. Once the reinforcer is freely accessible, then any intervening performance requirements are self-imposed. If a rat, after having received his food pellet, were to place it aside, jog twenty laps around his cage, and then consume his reward, we could talk of self-control.

The previously cited study by Powell and Azrin (1968) on smoking reduction provides a second illustration of the internal-external distinction. These workers designed a cigarette case that delivered a painful electric shock each time it was opened. Was their study an investigation of self-punishment? Not really, since the administration of shock was electromechanically controlled. That is, following the target behavior (i.e., reaching for a cigarette) the punitive consequences were automatically programmed. One could, of course, argue that the individual, being totally aware of the imminent consequences of his act, chose to engage in the target behavior and, therefore, was exhibiting a form of self-control. Such an interpretation poses problems when one considers the fact that many behavior patterns (particularly "habitual" ones) occur without cognitive awareness (Neisser, 1966). As Premack (1971) has pointed out, a smoker may reach for a cigarette without realizing either his actions or the consequences. One would certainly not want to argue that the proverbial rat—knowing impending consequences of his act—is exhibiting self-control when he chooses to press (or not to press) a lever for food. It is important to note that Powell and Azrin's subjects did engage in a self-control pattern when they optionally employed the specially designed cigarette case. That is, by carrying the case and restricting themselves to these cigarettes, they employed an environmental planning strategy. The cigarette case allowed them to prearrange the consequences of a target behavior. Interestingly, Powell and Azrin found that their subjects tended to use the shock case less and less frequently as the study progressed. This avoidance of using the special cigarette case might be said to be externally maintained.

A third illustration of the locus of control issue draws upon the use of drugs in self-control. Skinner (1953) has listed such behaviors as the ingestion of aphrodisiacs or anesthetics as possible forms of self-control (cf. Table 1–1). However, in terms of our internal–external analysis, such behaviors might be seen as *relatively* external in control. Anesthetics, for example, are reinforcing by themselves so one would hesitate to label their ingestion as self-control. There are, however, some drug-taking patterns that do involve self-regulation in a more direct manner. For example, a popular drug in the treatment of alcoholism is disulfiram (commercially known as Antabuse). When mixed with alcohol, disulfiram produces a mild poison that causes severe nausea and illness. Thus, once the drug has been ingested, the consequences of alcohol consumption have been prearranged. When the alcoholic optionally takes the drug he is exhibiting environmental self-control.

The foregoing discussion should re-emphasize the previously discussed reciprocity between internal and external control systems. Likewise, it should highlight the importance of minimizing external constraints in self-regulation research. While an experimenter may legitimately suggest or model various forms or standards of self-control, interpretations are complicated when an external agent controls self-administered consequences or schedules (e.g., Johnson & Martin, in press). Meaningful research on the processes of self-control requires that investigators minimize the frequency, magnitude, and immediacy of those external variables that frequently accompany self-regulatory situations. By measuring and controlling external factors, a more accurate estimate of self-control principles is made possible. Moreover, these controls are required if self-management findings are to be replicable.

EXTRANEOUS VARIABLES
IN SELF–CONTROL

There is now a substantial amount of evidence indicating that extraneous, or "nonspecific" variables, the second methodological issue, may account for a disturbing portion of the phenomena observed in psychological experimentation and therapy (cf. Orne, 1962; Rosenthal, 1966, 1967). Extraneous in the sense that they are usually outside the researcher's immediate interests, such variables have been the object of all too little effort with regard to regulation, particularly in the area of self-control. We will, therefore, briefly describe some of the more familiar variables in order to provide the necessary information for an understanding of our subsequent evaluation of self-control research.

Subject Selection Bias

Perhaps one of the more obvious variables that, if not extraneous, goes frequently uncontrolled in self-control research is that of subject selection bias. Admittedly, the researcher or clinician working in self-control often deals with a subsample of all subjects available to him—namely, those who have shown some "motivation" to regulate their own behavior (i.e., a commitment to change consisting of various internal processes such as self-thoughts and instructions). The presence of such motivation is perhaps less problematical than either its degree or type. That is, subjects frequently vary both in their degree of motivation to self-regulate and also in their cause of motivation (Marston & Feldman, 1972; Kanfer & Karoly, 1972a). A lung-cancer patient, for example, may find it easier to self-manage his smoking than someone who simply considers smoking a dirty habit. A more extreme illustration of possible motivational complications is provided in studies wherein the self-control subject is either the author himself (e.g., Roberts, 1969) or a member of his family (e.g.,

Nolan, 1968). While such reports are of value, their interpretation is complicated.

Expectation

A second source of "noise" in self-control research has to do with the power of suggestion. This variable is also called "expectancy," "demand characteristics," or the "placebo effect." A placebo is a harmless and inert drug (or therapeutic technique) that, despite its actual impotence, may effect in its recipient a therapeutic improvement whose degree and duration vary considerably. Psychologists have gradually come to realize that just about any technique can be partially and/or temporarily effective if it is presented with generous professional assurance and the expectancy of improvement. Thus, when a person seeks advice on his behavioral adjustment, he *expects* to be helped. If the therapist is enthusiastic and confident in his recommendation of a technique, the response set for improvement is also strengthened. This "willingness to be cured" has been frequently encountered in psychotherapy. A colleague once related how he had successfully treated an obsessive-compulsive woman by simply telling her to "STOP IT!" Most instances of therapeutic suggestion or placebo improvement are not quite as transparent, but their frequency is probably grossly underestimated (Frank, 1961). It is worth noting that the power of suggestion is not always therapeutic: For example, Bernstein (1970) reported that college students were much more fearful when their encounter with a rat was perceived as a "fear assessment" exercise rather than an "animal communication" experiment.

Placebo, expectancy, and suggestion effects are just as important in self-control research as in other areas of behavioral science (Jeffrey, 1974). These extraneous variables probably contribute to the effectiveness of many (if not all) self-regulatory strategies. Implicit experimenter communications may also be particularly important in self-management research (Orne, 1970). For example, to label a preintervention phase of data collection as a self-recorded "baseline" may very well generate the expectation that behavior changes should (or will) not occur until some "treatment" is introduced. If the processes and parameters of self-control are to be accurately estimated, the effects of these variables must be controlled and assessed (Nelson & McReynolds, 1971). McFall and Hammen (1971) have shown that motivated volunteering and a minimally structured "treatment" program may account for a sizeable portion of the results reported in the smoking control literature. Therefore, to assess the contribution of specific self-regulatory techniques when they are added to a background of nonspecific factors, the latter must be experimentally isolated (e.g., via control groups) so that evaluative comparisons can be made.

Reactivity of Self-Observation

A third type of variable, that of self-observation (although not extraneous to self-control research), has been virtually ignored until recently. When an individual attends to, records, or otherwise observes his own behavior, there is often a subsequent change in that behavior (cf. Kazdin, 1974). This strikingly simple principle has, nevertheless, been frequently overlooked in the design and execution of self-control research (e.g., Lawson & May, 1970). Thus it is very likely that the use of self-observation "control groups" to the exclusion of all others has led to the underestimation of treatment effectiveness. That self-observation may constitute one of the more active ingredients in at least some types of self-control is indicated by McFall and Hammen's (1971) analysis of smoking control variables. At this point self-control researchers using self-observation would do well to partial out its effects before drawing any conclusions. The conceptualization and evidence bearing on self-observation effects will be explored more fully in Chapter 3.

The foregoing discussion has focused on a few of the more common variables often overlooked or uncontrolled in self-management research. The list is probably an infinite one. However, it is felt that the former are probably among the more reactive in terms of their contribution to self-control effects.

EXPERIMENTAL DESIGN IN SELF–CONTROL RESEARCH

The third methodological issue, experimental design, is another area that needs further study. Although few psychologists would dispute the importance of self-control processes in human functioning, there has been a distressing absence of hard empirical evidence in this area (Mahoney, 1972a). With the exception of a few laboratory studies and a handful of well-executed field experiments, much of the theorizing in self-control has been based on speculation, extrapolation from other fields, or the minimal data provided by unreplicated case histories. Intensive studies of individual self-control applications do, of course, provide valuable information on the power of specific techniques. However, when unreplicated or poorly executed, such studies provide only tentative (and perhaps misleading) information.

It might be worthwhile at this point to comment on empirical standards in self-control research. One of the contemporary criticisms of "hardnosed" experimental approaches to human behavior is that they tend to ignore and degrade the overwhelming complexities of human functioning. Some behavioral scientists are criticized for their avoidance of subjective (private) data and their glorification of trite experimental methodologies or designs (Maslow, 1966). Arnold Lazarus, an esteemed contributor to the application of behavior principles in the clinical realm, has also voiced some objections to the steadfast exclusion and/or denigration of data from anything but rigorously polished experimental studies (Lazarus, 1971a, 1971b; Lazarus & Davison, 1971). Lazarus' argument for the use of clinical data (as contrasted to that derived from well-controlled laboratory studies) is perhaps both appropriate and timely. However, case studies that rely heavily on subjective impressions of improvement can only provide illustrative directives for further research and applications. That is, unless an individual case history is executed with an eye for objective (and operational) data collection plus experimental control, its contribution of clinical information must be considered limited until independent replication provides further support. While there may be no absolute standards for empirical research in any field, including self-control, some considerations must be made in the interpretation of data. Different degrees of confidence are warranted by different types of data (Kaplan, 1964). A subjective "clinical impression" is a datum less deserving of confidence until its utility (i.e., reliability and validity) can be independently demonstrated. In general, the degree of confidence assigned to a particular set of self-control data is enhanced by each of the following:

1. an explicit definition of both the behavior to be changed and the technique employed;
2. independent observation of the targeted behavior so that subjects' self-reports can be substantiated;
3. independent observation of the self-control operation;
4. an assessment of the target behavior in both the presence and absence of the self-regulatory technique (e.g., via control groups, reversals, pre/post measures, etc.);
5. the presence of long-term follow-up data;
6. at least one replication (preferably independent); and
7. attention to the control of extraneous independent variables (demand characteristics, expectation, experimenter bias, etc.).

The absence of any or all of the above does not, of course, mean that a set of data is useless or without meaning to self-control workers. It is important, however, to realize that the scientific rationale is a multicomponent approach with degrees. The components enumerated above have shown themselves to be useful guidelines in the interpretation of empirical research.

There are two fundamental types of experimental studies that are frequently encountered in self-control research. The first—called the *empirical case study*—deals with one subject at a time. The second—the *empirical group study*—involves groups of subjects. Each design tends to answer different kinds of questions. Their major differences involve how individual variability is conceptualized and treated, and the relative importance of experimental versus statistical control (Thoresen, in press).

The Empirical Case Study

The intensive study of individual subjects is a common strategy in self-control research. In this approach, the behavior of a single subject is observed and evaluated in the presence of one or more variables of interest (Sidman, 1960; Chassan, 1967; Browning & Stover, 1971). In order to assess the effects of a particular self-control strategy, a comparison must be made between measurements of a target behavior in both the presence and absence of that strategy. That is, the influence of a smoking control technique can only be evaluated if one has an index of smoking rate both before and after the implementation of the technique.

Several different experimental designs have been employed in empirical case studies (cf. Sidman, 1960; Helmstadter, 1970; Wolf & Risley, 1971; Thoresen, in press). By far the most popular has been that labeled *operant reversal*, or the *ABAB design* (the name derived from its phases). In this strategy, a behavior is first observed and recorded in the absence of any treatment variables (this *A* phase is termed "baseline"). Then a treatment is introduced (Phase *B* or "intervention"), and the behavior continues to be measured so that any changes can be evaluated. Thereafter, the original pretreatment conditions are reinstated ("reversal" to Phase *A* again) and, finally, the treatment conditions are resumed (Phase *B* or "reintervention"). The reversal to original conditions is performed partly to show that any observed changes in behavior co-vary with the presence of the treatment variable (thereby controlling for such extraneous factors as maturation). The reversal and reintervention also provide a replication of the relationship under study.

Although ABAB designs have been used by a few self-control researchers (e.g., Glynn, 1970; Axelrod, Hall, Weis, & Rohrer, 1974), they pose the problem of behavioral reversibility (cf. Sidman, 1960). Some behaviors, such as reading or other cognitive skills, are unlikely to return to baseline frequencies when their training conditions are removed. More pertinent to self-control, however, is the fact that individuals may strongly object to "reversing" to pretreatment conditions after they have executed a successful self-control program. The formerly obese subject, for example, might be understandably reluctant to regain hard-lost pounds simply to satisfy the scientist's definition of well-executed research.

A second design, an alternative to the ABAB, elimates the need for reversals. In this *multiple-baseline design*, baseline data are collected on two or more behaviors simultaneously. Thereafter, each behavior is sequentially modified. For example, if four personal hygiene behaviors have been recorded for a baseline period, the first (e.g., nailbiting) might be treated for several weeks while the other three remain untreated. Then the second response (e.g., toothbrushing) would be added to the currently-under-treatment category and treated while the remaining two remain untreated. Then the third and, somewhat later, the fourth behaviors would receive treatment. This strategy of staggered or sequential interventions provides a powerful means of assessing the effectiveness of a technique: Behaviors not yet treated provide both a cumulative baseline index and a continuing control for extraneous variables. Moreover, each successive intervention provides a replication of the relationship under study. The Morganstern (in press) study presented in Chapter 5 illustrates this feature. Multiple-baseline designs for comparisons between subjects and situations have also been reported (Kazdin, 1972).

The advantages of the multiple-baseline design have, unfortunately, been overlooked by many self-control researchers. There are, of course, several disadvantages that limit its usefulness. For one thing, at least two behaviors may be needed for comparative replication. If the behaviors are related, a change in one may influence the other. Moreover, when the behaviors of interest vary widely in frequency or type, then the multiple-baseline design may be at a disadvantage. Finally, when two or more different forms of treatment are separately employed (e.g., Mahoney, 1971), then the multiple-baseline design provides its control function without any replication. Overall, however, self-control researchers would do well to consider the many advantages of the multiple-baseline design over no-baseline or ABAB strategies.

A third experimental design appropriate for self-control research has been labeled the *changing criterion design* (Axelrod, Hall, Weis, & Rohrer, 1974). In this design a certain treatment is introduced in successively varied amounts, and causality is inferred from co-variations between responses and the value of the treatment variable. For example, Axelrod *et al.* instructed a subject to impose successively more stringent limits on his smoking behavior. These researchers found a correlation of .73 between daily smoking rate and this self-imposed ceiling. Similarly, Mahoney and Bandura (1972) showed that a pigeon's response rate co-varied significantly with a successively increased standard for self-reward. Note that this feature provides numerous partial replications of the relationship under study. While the changing criterion design is not optimal in its control over possible extraneous factors, it does provide the opportunity for assessment of successively modified treatment interventions. Since many behavior modification strategies incorporate a gradual response approximation feature, the changing criterion design could prove particularly useful in their analysis.

It should be mentioned that, although the above designs are predominantly employed with a single subject, they can also be used with two subjects or groups (Gottman, 1973). Moreover, the role of intrasubject replications should not be confused with that of intersubject replications. An ABAB analysis of some technique, for example, may show replication of the effects of Condition *B* within a particular subject (intrasubject). When that relationship is observed in one or more other subjects, then intersubject replication is involved. Both of these forms of replication are important in self-control research: Intrasubject replicability adds to our confidence that a specific set of treatment conditions was responsible for some observed change. Intersubject replicability, in addition, provides information on the generality of the relationship to other persons.

There are, of course, many other single-subject designs that fit a wide range of research needs. Browning and Stover (1971) and Thoresen (in press) provide excellent summaries of these variations. Glass, Willson, and Gottman (1972) also discuss variations as well as data analysis techniques for intensive designs. The above three designs, however, constitute those most frequently encountered in empirical case studies.

Finally, brief mention should be made of the relative advantages and disadvantages of single-subject designs in self-control research. First, the empirical case study provides invaluable data on response trends, or "transition states" (cf. Sidman, 1960). By intensively studying the moment-to-moment responding of one person at a time, important information can be obtained on such things as rate changes and multiprocess responding. While group studies could gather similar data, they have customarily used only pre- and post-measurements (thereby ignoring many intervening processes). One disadvantage of single-subject designs is that they require many systematic replications for the empirical comparison of two or more techniques. For such a comparison, the techniques in question must be applied separately to the same behavior. For example, one might wish to compare the effectiveness of self-reward and self-punishment techniques in helping one's mother-in-law lose weight. After noting a baseline index of her weight, one could suggest one technique and implement it for several weeks. After a reversal to baseline conditions, the second technique could be implemented. One's conclusions from such a strategy, however, are greatly limited by the fact that the same subject has experienced a particular sequence of treatments. Consequently, the effectiveness of one technique may be substantially altered by its having been preceded by some other technique. Perhaps our subject would have done better if self-reward had preceded self-punishment as a treatment strategy. Moreover, if one were interested in making generalizations about the two techniques, numerous subjects would have to be tested. Despite these possible drawbacks, many researchers have supported the practical utility and scientific power of single-subject designs (Thoresen, in press).

The empirical case study is an invaluable design for the controlled demonstration of a therapeutic effect. In individual clinical instances in which neither generalizability nor treatment comparisons are of prime interest, intensive study of the single subject offers a powerful as well as practical format.

The Empirical Group Study

Investigations employing groups of subjects also seek to compare behavioral differences in the presence and absence of certain variables. In contrast to the empirical case study, which makes such comparisons within a single subject, group studies expose different groups of subjects to varying degrees of a treatment variable. For example, a single-subject ABAB analysis of the effectiveness of self-punishment on smoking behavior would entail a comparison of one person's smoking rate both in the presence and the absence of self-punishment. An empirical group approach to this same problem might entail two relatively similar groups of smokers, asking one group to self-punish while the second (control) group continued without treatment. Often there will be several treatment groups—each receiving some unique type or combination of therapeutic techniques—and several control groups—each containing factors whose effects are to be used for comparison. An empirical group study might, for example, compare the effects of several self-control strategies to the effects of such things as expectation of improvement or no treatment at all.

One of the more crucial factors in the evaluation of group-based research is whether adequate control groups have been employed. For example, if one were to read a study reporting substantial weight loss on the part of subjects who charted and rewarded their dietetic progress, the interpretation of these results would weigh heavily on at least two comparisons: (1) How did the above subjects compare with subjects who simply charted their progress, and (2) how did they compare with subjects who engaged in neither self-charting nor self-reward? The results of a study are more easily interpretable when any and all possible independent variables have been isolated. If Factor A had no effect, but Factor B did (either in a separate group or when combined with A), then we have some indication that B is the active ingredient.

The relative advantages and disadvantages of empirical group studies have already been briefly touched on. Group studies allow one not only to evaluate the effectiveness of a specific technique but also permit comparisons among various techniques. There are, of course, the drawbacks that, at least traditionally, group studies have paid little attention to moment-to-moment behavior changes or individual variations in responding. These problems can, however, be attenuated by appropriate use of trend analyses and the reporting of individual as well as group performance data. The various designs and rationale of group studies are well summarized by Campbell and Stanley (1966).

RELIABILITY AND VALIDITY
IN SELF–CONTROL

A fourth methodological issue in self-control research concerns the reliability and validity of self-reported data. Despite the fact that many investigators employ changes in subjects' self-reports as their sole dependent variable, there have been distressingly few attempts to corroborate the honesty and accuracy of such reports (Simkins, 1971a). Without such checks, the self-control researcher is totally at the mercy of subjects' self-reports. This, in turn, introduces the serious possibility of an experimenter's unwitting alteration of verbal self-reports (e.g., via differential reinforcement or covert communication) without having correspondingly altered the behavior in question.

Before pursuing the methodological issue, a few definitions are in order. *Reliability* refers to the consistency of a measurement. For example, a bathroom scale may repeatedly register the same weight when a person steps on and off it several times. However, even though the same weight has been consistently registered each time, that weight may be inaccurate (e.g., two pounds heavy). *Validity* refers to the "true" accuracy of a measurement regardless of its consistency. There is, of course, a relationship between validity and reliability. As we shall see, self-report validity may be the relatively more important issue in self-regulation. Jeffrey (1974) and Kazdin (1974) present an excellent discussion of possible validity problems in self-management.

The admittedly meager evidence currently available on self-reports indicates considerable intersubject variability. Again, this emphasizes the need for reliability and validity estimates in self-control research. The naive assumption that highly motivated subjects will be both consistent and accurate in their self-reporting is not supported by the available evidence. Herbert and Baer (1972) reported little agreement between highly motivated mothers observing their own behavior with their child and data from external observers. Thoresen *et al.* (1973, in press) also found marked discrepancies between the self-observations of a nursery-school teacher and external observers. Fixsen, Phillips, and Wolf (1972) discovered that adolescent boys are far from being "naturally accurate" observers of their own behaviors. These same investigators showed that the validity of self-reports can be enhanced by providing training in the discrimination and labeling of the behavior in question and also by imposing positive consequences for self-report accuracy.

The fact that self-observation training was required to obtain respectable correspondence between self-reports and observer reports is worth noting. Even though many behavior modifiers go to great pains to train accurate observers of others' behaviors, they frequently seem to assume that the individual is an expert in self-observation. Again, this assumption appears to be untenable in light of data cited above.

Some researchers have also found that self-reporting is often initially inaccurate but modifiable. Risley and Hart (1968), for example, showed that preschool children are very responsive to reinforcement contingencies that bear on self-report accuracy. When children were rewarded for self-reports of a certain play activity, the verbal self-reports increased in frequency without any changes in the actual behavior reported upon. However, when rewards were made contingent on a correspondence between the children's self-reports and their previous play activities, high correlations developed. This study exemplifies the important distinction between the self-report as a verbal behavior and the actual behavior reported. Changes in the one need not be associated with changes in the other. Another study that corroborated the modifiability of self-report accuracies is that of Bolstad and Johnson (1972). Using contingent points (redeemable for prizes) to encourage accurate self-reports of classroom behaviors in first- and second-graders, they found considerable correspondence with the records of an independent observer. Flowers (1972) has also demonstrated that accurate self-monitoring is a skill requiring both training and maintenance incentives. Viewing self-observation as a learned skill,

"165—See there, I haven't gained a pound since the day we were married!"

Thoresen and his colleagues (Hendricks, Thoresen, & Hubbard, 1973) are developing a training program to teach accurate and reliable self-observation behaviors.

It should, perhaps, be mentioned that variations in the reliability and validity of self-reports may also reflect differing types of self-observation. For example, some researchers require subjects to use actuarial recording of some targeted behavior (i.e., counting each separate occurrence of the response), while others (e.g., Mahoney, 1971) have employed a time-sampling format. The correspondence between self-reports and observer reports may vary as a function of the similarity of the two recording systems; Broden, Hall, and Mitts (1971) report poor day-to-day self-report accuracies in two eighth-grade students, but good correspondence between overall averages for one subject. Likewise, the difficulty of the self-observation may vary. In the study reported by Fixsen, Phillips, and Wolf (1972), the adolescent boys were required to learn a list of twenty-one very complex operational definitions. Finally, the reliability of self-reports may vary when subjective frequency estimates are employed rather than actual behavior samples (e.g., Goldstein, 1966).

Several studies have indicated that self-reports are sometimes very consistent with external records. Axelrod, Hall, Weis, and Rohrer (1974) reported 100 percent correspondence between self-reports and independent observer records in two case studies involving smoking reduction. Similarly, other investigators (e.g., Ober, 1968: 94 percent) have found high accuracies in the self-recording of smoking. McFall (1970) found considerable variability in the correspondence between self-reported and externally recorded smoking frequency (range of correlations $= -.05$ to 1.00; mean $= .61$; correlation of mean frequency $= .96$). In a study on the improvement of regular self-medication, Azrin and Powell (1969) found a 98 percent agreement between self-reported and peer-reported time of medication. Mahoney, Moore, Wade, and Moura (1973) reported a high correlation (93.8 percent) between actual and self-recorded instances of correct problem solving in an academic review task. Finally, Hall (1972) found an average correlation of .91 between women's self-reported weights and actual weekly measurements.

The above findings suggest that accurate self-reporting, while certainly not an inherent talent, can be established and enhanced by appropriate training and feedback. In several of the studies that reported high correspondence between self-records and external records, subjects had the foreknowledge that their accuracy and honesty would be checked. Moreover, in some instances (e.g., Ober, 1968; Powell & Azrin, 1968; Chapman, Smith, & Layden, 1971), subjects were allowed to choose the individual who would gather accuracy data on their self-reports. This, unfortunately, suggests the possibility that a form of discrimination training may have been involved. There is now some preliminary evidence indicating that observers are more accurate when they know their reliability is being checked and less accurate soon after such a check (Reid, 1970). Alternatively, when subjects can choose their own independent observer, it is likely that they will choose one who might be less than objective. Therefore, in addition to the provision of training in accurate self-recording, self-control researchers would do well to consider the use of unobtrusive measures of self-report accuracies (cf. Webb, Campbell, Schwartz, & Sechrest, 1966). These measures are readily incorporated into laboratory studies (cf. Mahoney, Moore, Wade, & Moura, 1973) but may require more ingenuity for naturalistic applications. For example, grade-point averages might be used to corroborate self-reported study improvements, and reductions in dental plaque might provide some gross corroboration of smoking changes.

The foregoing findings also have direct bearing on those self-control situations wherein direct validity estimates are impossible. For example, when the behavior to be self-regulated is covert (e.g., obsessions, urges, and self-evaluative thoughts), then independent checks are more complicated. In addition, such situations make the training of accurate self-reporting much more difficult (Skinner, 1953, 1963, 1969). When the covert behavior is directly linked to an overt response pattern (as in obsessions and compulsions or urges and actions), then indirect evidence on changes in the former can be obtained from changes in the latter. However, one must be careful in any such inference due to the potential independence of self-reports and target behaviors (Risley & Hart, 1968; Nelson & McReynolds, 1971; Simkins, 1971b). Preliminary data have shown that indirect reliability estimates can be obtained for some covert behaviors (e.g., Mahoney, Thoresen, & Danaher, 1972), and that, once again, subjects vary considerably in their accuracy.

Overall, the sobering empirical complications involved in the self-reporting and self-regulation of covert behaviors should not discourage their continued investigation. Covert responses are, after all, no less "scientific" than their overt counterparts (Kaplan, 1964; Mahoney, 1970; Day, 1971; Thoresen, 1973) and play a very significant role in complex human functioning. Their analysis and regulation pose one of the more exciting challenges to self-control researchers. Investigators in this area would do well, however, to attend very conscientiously to the elimination or control of all extraneous variables (e.g., demand characteristics) that might account for some effect. Due to the fact that all evidence on covert self-control is indirect and/or inferential, one's confidence in such evidence may be somewhat less than when overt behaviors are involved. Independent replications and well-controlled inquiries are, therefore, all the more crucial for the evaluation and interpretation of self-reported changes in covert responses. Given some of the methodological difficulties in this area, preliminary investigations have shown covert self-control to be a very promising area for therapeutically relevant research (see Chapter 6).

One final point regarding the reliability and validity issue in self-control concerns the consistency with which some self-regulatory strategy is implemented. Just as it is important to corroborate a subject's data on the frequency of some target behavior, it is, likewise, imperative that an index of his "follow-through" be obtained. If a person has been told to self-punish his smoking by tearing up a dollar bill after every cigarette, we need to assess not only the accuracy of his self-reported smoking data, but also his consistency in employing the prescribed self-management strategy. One might otherwise conclude that such a strategy was ineffective when, in fact, it was simply never applied. The importance of this type of data cannot be overemphasized. It makes little difference whether some technique *would* be effective *if* implemented when such implementation is either nonexistent or not evaluated. Moreover, the "contract problem" (getting a person to adhere to some self-regulatory commitment) may never be solved unless follow-through data are collected. Existing evidence on follow-through would seem to implicate external variables as important factors affecting the consistent use of self-control operations (e.g., Kanfer, Cox, Greiner, & Karoly, 1972; Mahoney, Moura, & Wade, 1973). The contract problem will be discussed in more detail in Chapter 5. Note, however, that the analysis of a self-regulatory technique requires that the technique be appropriately self-applied. The latter, in turn, can only be evaluated if data are gathered on operational follow-through. While field studies often complicate the collection of consistency data in self-control operations (cf. Powell & Azrin, 1968; Azrin & Powell, 1969), a portion of the latter can be restricted to an experimenter-monitored situation so that at least a partial assessment can be made.

The present chapter has explored some of the methodological issues that face self-control researchers. Needless to say, the investigation of self-regulatory phenomena requires considerable sophistication in experimental methods (and, perhaps, an exceptional tolerance for frustration). The fact that some preliminary research on self-control has overlooked important methodological factors should not discourage attempts to enhance the quality of subsequent inquiries. Judging from the existing evidence supporting the therapeutic promise of systematic self-regulation, continuing research efforts will be amply rewarded.

Chapter

3

Self-Observation

The concepts of awareness, insight, and consciousness are at the heart of every major psychotherapeutic system. Psychoanalytic strategies have emphasized awareness of historical antecedents and the developmental etiology of "symptoms." Freud argued that the awareness of past events could lead to immediate changes in behavior. Rogers (1961) stressed awareness of what the person is *currently* experiencing. Such awareness is considered prerequisite to accepting and understanding oneself. Yoga and Zen have also highlighted the focusing of attention on inner experience such as thoughts and physical reactions. The task is to become aware of these internal actions, the "on-going present" (e.g., Watts, 1961).

Behavioral approaches have also emphasized insight and awareness but of a different sort. Instead of stressing the interpretations of historical antecedents or global focusing on the "here and now," behavioral approaches have stressed the importance of examining the antecedents and consequences of certain actions. Awareness as such comes about by studying how a certain behavior is influenced.

Benjamin Franklin was probably one of the first persons to use behavioral self-observation. He identified thirteen response areas ("virtues") that he wanted to increase ("acquire the habitude of"). Franklin wrote:

> I judged it would be well not to distract my attention by attempting the whole at once, but to fix it on one of them at a time; and, when I should be master of that, then to proceed to another. . . . Conceiving, then, that daily examination would be necessary, I contrived the following method for conducting that examination. I made a book, in which I allotted a page for each of the virtues. I ruled each page with red ink, so as to have seven columns, one for each day of the week, marking each column with a letter for the day. I crossed these columns with thirteen red lines, marking the beginning of each line with the first letter of one of the virtues, on which line, and in its proper column, I might mark by a little black spot every fault I found upon examination to have been committed respecting that virtue upon that day. . . .

Behavioral approaches share much in common with the humanistic and Eastern strategies in emphasizing the current environment and in focusing on what the person is doing in everyday life situations (Buhler, 1971). However, the similarity quickly fades in that behavioral strategies emphasize systematic gathering of data on specific actions by the therapist or client. Self-control strategies place primary reliance on self-observation as the *first* major step in programs for self-change. In the self-control systems model that we have presented, the systematic gathering of data is the life blood of effective self-control methods. The person must first know what is happening *before* any self-change program is initiated. Often, the person may find that his self-collected data reveal something very different from his first impressions.

Behavioral researchers have recently recognized the singular importance of self-observation as a performance in its own right. Having a person systematically collect data on his own actions has been viewed as something more than a methodological technique in the traditional scientific sense. The unique characteristic of the human organism, as Tielhard de Chardin (1959) once observed, appears to be that a person "knows that he knows." That is, as an individual gathers information about his own actions, such information may influence the very action being observed. One of the main problems of systematic self-observation is that such procedures serve both as a method of gathering performance data as well as a possible self-change technique. In this respect, self-observation presents methodological and conceptual problems similar to those encountered with small particles in physics (e.g., Heisenberg's principle of indeterminacy and Bohr's work in complementarity). The act of observing a phenomenon may drastically alter that phenomenon; the process of measurement interacts to influence the object of measurement. With self-observation the person is the observer and the observed. Some physical scientists (Whitehead, 1925; Bridgman, 1959; Matson, 1964; Blackburn, 1971) have argued that in studying human behavior the classical notions of objectivity, reliability, and experimental methodology must be expanded to account for human phenomena in more valid ways. In particular, reliance on the individual person as a source of data by means of his own sensory and perceptual skills has been recommended. The detached observer approach has been criticized as too one-sided and as perpetuating the artificial dualism between mind and body that has dominated western science (Tart, 1972). The need for a more interdependent approach that stresses the continuum of all kinds of human behavior is emphasized here. This is especially true in trying to understand the processes and effects of self-observation.

AN ANALYSIS OF
SELF–OBSERVATION

Self-observation is a highly complex process involving both covert and overt behaviors. Further, while self-observation is discussed separately from self-controlling techniques such as self-reinforcement and self-punishment, the intimate interaction between such processes should be acknowledged. Self-observation does not function in any pure or independent sense. As already mentioned, the person knows that he knows. This knowledge is "unusual" in the sense that much human behavior is automatic and nonconscious. Viewed as an operant, self-observation can be triggered by interoceptive (digestive, respiratory, circulatory), proprioceptive (muscles, body movement), and exteroceptive (other persons, physical events) cues; that is, stimuli from within and from without. These cues occur when something happens that interferes with the typically automatic functioning of the person. Kanfer (1970a) has suggested that certain discrepancies take place that arouse the person to take note of what is happening. For instance, certain interventions by others may prompt the person to self-observe—a wife's angry comment, the seductive stare of an attractive person, the boss's threat of punishment. Physiological changes within the body can provide cues as can certain self-verbalizations (thoughts) and images. A person's worrying about a forthcoming event (e.g., a public speech) or imagining a very pleasant past experience can trigger self-observation. The unexpected (e.g., failure of predicted results to occur) typically encourages some kind of self-observation as do decision situations where the person must make one of several possible responses. In effect, any internal or external event that arouses the organism sets the occasion for self-observation.

Given this arousal or disruption from the usually automatic ways of behaving, what does the person do? Eastern techniques such as yoga and Zen would seek to reduce nonconscious or automatic behavior across the board, toward a life style that accentuates total awareness of the ongoing present. Contemporary sensitivity and encounter methods would seek an expanded general awareness of sensory and cognitive actions, in part through external feedback (i.e., the comments of others). The behavioral perspective offered here, however, suggests that the person must learn specific self-observation techniques through systematic learning experiences. Such techniques not only make the person aware but give him pinpointed information to use in making decisions about what to do.

Discrimination

What does a person do when he makes a self-observation? First, some type of discrimination is required: The individual must discern the presence or absence of a particular response, be it a positive self-thought, a hand gesture, or the smoking of a cigarette. This discrimination is best thought of as a behavior or response in itself, functionally similar to other instrumental responses and under the control of internal and external stimuli. For example, a sharp pain in the back of the neck can serve as a discriminative stimulus "telling" the person that he is feeling very tense. The facial expression of a close friend can provide a cue as well. Hence self-observation first requires some type of discriminative response that is, itself, under the control of a covert or overt cue.

Several explanations exist as to how this discriminative behavior is learned. Skinner (1953) has suggested that these discriminations are learned at an early age from the person's social environment, especially through the verbal behavior of parents, siblings, and others. This rationale has been expanded recently by Staats (1971) and others (e.g., Thoresen, 1973a). Discriminative responses also appear to relate to theory and research in self-perception and attribution (Lefcourt, 1966; Schachter, 1966; Nisbett & Valins, 1971; Valins & Nisbett, 1971; Bem, 1972).

A discriminative response can be thought of as the awareness facet of self-observation (Ferster, 1972). However, being aware in a discriminative sense may not provide the detailed information necessary to implement a self-control program. Knowing, for example, that one is feeling anxious does not necessarily provide the detail needed to understand the antecedents and consequences that may be causing that anxiety. Discrimination must be followed by some kind of recording procedure so that the occurrence of the behavior can be viewed in a systematic way. One of the major differences between humanistic-sensitivity-awareness approaches and behavioral ones is that the former seldom take the next step beyond discrimination and self-awareness, namely, systematic recording and alteration of responses. Further, the discriminations are typically so global and nonspecific that it is difficult to pinpoint and, therefore, to alter their occurrence.

Recording and Charting

The second process of self-observation has to do with the systematic recording of the observed response. Some methods of recording self-observations will be discussed shortly. Questions arise such as when and how often to record the observed behavior: Should the observation take place immediately afterwards or at the end of the day or week; should the unit of self-observation be somewhat general or highly specific? The timing of the self-observation may be an important factor. For example, recording the urge to have a cigarette may disrupt the behavioral chain sufficiently to prevent the smoking from occurring (McFall, 1970). Obviously the recording of having smoked a cigarette after the fact cannot disrupt that particular event, although it may influence subsequent smoking.

The relative effects of using separate or combined methods of recording remain unknown. However, translating self-recorded data into some form of visual display (e.g., a chart) may set the occasion for possible reinforcing consequences from the environment. For instance, a weight chart in the bathroom can readily be observed by other members of the family and may prompt compliments or criticisms, depending on the progress displayed. Some studies have used this "public" charting as a way of changing the external environment to promote desired behavior (e.g., Rutner & Bugle, 1969). A deliberate display of progress early in a self-change program can elicit powerful support and encouragement from the environment (Thoresen, 1973b).

Evaluation and Goal-Setting

Coupled with the discrimination and recording of a response is evaluation or what may be called the *data analysis phase*. Here the person examines his self-observation data. Such an examination can provide a basis for self-evaluation, which, in turn, can lead to self-reinforcement (Kanfer, 1971). The individual's evaluation of his data is stressed here because it plays a crucial part in the technology of teaching behavioral self-control. Errors about what the charted data represent can seriously hinder success in self-control.

Kolb, Winter, and Berlew (1968) examined the behavior change influence of self-observation coupled with individual goal-setting. These authors asked graduate students to set goals for changing their own behavior. Each person observed behaviors relevant to that goal and kept daily charts. For ten weeks a series of weekly meetings was held for the fifty-four students involved. Half of the students were encouraged to discuss their progress in each session, and group members were encouraged to provide one another with feedback. This feedback condition was contrasted to the other half of the students, who met in group meetings but did not discuss their individual projects. The results indicated that there was more change for those persons who received feedback (social reinforcement) on their self-reported progress. Unfortunately, the effects of self-observation and goal-setting are obscured by social reinforcement effects and the absence of appropriate control groups.

Subsequent research in the area of obesity has suggested that goal-setting and self-evaluation may not enhance performance in some self-monitoring situations (Mahoney, 1972b; Mahoney, Moura, & Wade, 1973). There is reason to believe, however, that achievement goals or standards contribute significantly to the performance of a wide range of social, academic, and cognitive behaviors (Locke, Cartledge, & Koeppel, 1968; Kanfer, 1971). Bandura (1971b) has observed that unrealistic goal-setting is a frequent concomitant of depression and extreme behavior pathology. The frequent use of both implicit and explicit goals in self-control endeavors argues for more controlled inquiries in this area.

METHODS OF SELF–OBSERVATION

At present, the technology for self-observation remains relatively crude and unexamined. A variety of devices has been used, such as wrist counters, pocket counters, wrist pads, booklets, and 3" × 5" cards. Video tapes have also been employed (Moore, Chernell, & West, 1965; Boyd & Sisney, 1967; Walz & Johnson, 1963; Stoller, 1968; Thomas, 1971; Kagan, 1972). The possibilities of self-recording devices are limited only by the creativity and imagination of prospective users.

One of the most popular self-observing devices is the wrist counter. Developed originally for use by golfers, the wrist counter was adapted by Lindsley (1968) for use as a counter in classroom and home environments. Multiple wrist counters can be worn by the individual when several behaviors are involved (e.g., Hannum, Thoresen, & Hubbard, 1974). Knitting tallies have also been used because they fit readily on pencils.

Other self-observation methods have employed various kinds of tally sheets and booklets. Figure 3–1, for example, presents samples from a booklet used by the authors in a field experiment concerning positive and

	AM	PM	AM	PM	AM	PM
12						
1						
2						
3						
4						
5						
6						
7						
8						
9						
10						
11						

Date	Significant Events

Figure 3–1   Sample pages from a self-monitoring diary. Occurrences of the behavior can be recorded on the first form and relevant events on the second form.

negative self-thoughts. An "all-or-none" recording system was used. If at least one negative self-thought occurred during an hour-long interval, an N was marked. This averted the complications of counting every single behavior (e.g., discriminating when one thought ended and the next began). By calculating the percentage of intervals during which the behavior occurred and examining their temporal distribution, valuable information was obtained.

Figure 3–2 presents a daily weight chart used in a weight reduction study (Mahoney, 1972b). Here the person weighs himself at approximately the same time each day and then records the net gain or loss relative to the preceding day. If a person is losing weight the connected dots for each day will present a descending line; if weight increases occur, an ascending line will be shown.

Another method of self-observation involves "countoons." Countoons have been developed for use by classroom teachers as well as by students themselves as part of a general approach to classroom learning called *precision teaching* (cf. Kunzelmann, 1970). The countoon has three basic components: (1) the *What I Do* picture sequence, (2) the *My Count* column, and (3) a *What Happens* column. Figure 3–3 presents an exam-

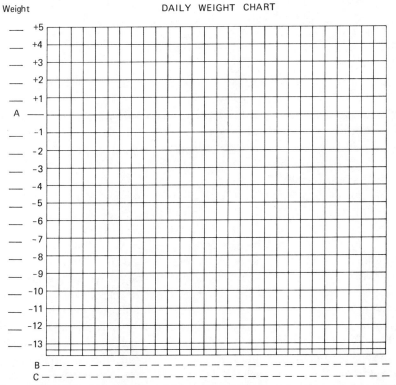

Figure 3–2   Record your daily weight on the above chart for the next four weeks. Weigh yourself at approximately the same time each day, making sure that you are wearing approximately the same amount of clothing each time. Vertical lines in the chart represent different days; horizontal lines represent the gain or loss of a pound. Begin by placing your present weight on Line A. Under the column marked "Weight," write what your actual weight would be if you lost 1 lb, 2 lbs, etc. On Line B write the first letter of each day of the week, beginning with today and, below it, on Line C the corresponding date. To chart your weight, place your finger on your present weight and then move across the page to the vertical line representing today. Your finger will be at an intersection of the two lines; mark it with a dot. If you had weighed yourself the previous day, you would now connect the two dots. The line will slant downward if you have lost weight, it will stay level if your weight is the same, or it will rise if you have gained.

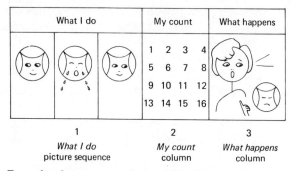

Figure 3–3   Example of a countoon for a child with a crying problem. (Adapted from H. Kunzelmann (Ed.), *Precision Teaching*, Seattle: Wash.: Special Child Publications, 1970, 290. Reproduced with permission.)

ple of a countoon for a child with a crying problem (Kunzelmann, 1970, p. 108). The division of the behavior sequence into three parts emphasizes what the person is doing just *before* the behavior occurs, the behavior itself, and the actions of the person *after* the behavior occurs. The cartoonlike stick figures are followed by the self-recording part, *My Count*. Here the child draws a circle around the number that indicates how often the behavior has occurred.

At present the technology of self-observation remains primitive. Little is known about the specific effects of certain kinds of self-monitoring devices, some of which have been described above. It seems reasonable that the method for recording and charting behaviors can interact with the environment to influence the behavior under observation. If the recording device is very apparent to other persons in the individual's daily life, then it is likely that the actions of these other people may influence the behavior being observed by the person. Such an influence may or may not be desirable. At this stage, however, small unobtrusive devices seem preferable. Further, such devices should provide a cumulative frequency of the behavior to permit the individual to chart readily the total frequencies for a given time period such as a day. The wrist counter seems to be ideally suited as an economical, convenient, and fairly unobtrusive self-recording device. Studies are needed, however, to evaluate the relative effects of using wrist counters and other devices on particular behaviors and in specified settings.

STUDIES OF SELF—OBSERVATION

Careful empirical studies of factors involved in self-observation have only recently been reported, and most of them have raised far more questions than they have answered. A basic problem in the few studies reported to date is that of confounding self-observation with other change processes. Often, for example, a self-observing subject may also receive external reinforcement for reporting progress. In addition, demand characteristics, experimental reactivity, and expectancy effects are frequent components in self-observation research (McFall, 1970; Jeffrey, 1974; Kazdin, 1974). To what extent is the person complying with the experimental situation to give the researcher what he is looking for? The subject may increase or decrease a certain observed behavior because of the strong expectancy created at the beginning of the study. It is not uncommon for therapists to tell clients that observing and recording their own actions will have a positive therapeutic effect. Sometimes continuing therapy has been made contingent on the client engaging in self-observation (Krumboltz & Thoresen, 1969). These factors are not a problem in the clinical sense if the behavior is being altered in the desired direction. Nevertheless, they do present problems for the clinician-researcher who is trying to evaluate the specific contributions of self-monitoring techniques.

Studies have been reported using self-observation procedures in combination with other behavior change strategies (e.g., Ferster, Nurnberger, & Levitt, 1962; Fox, 1962; Goldiamond, 1965a; Rehm & Marston, 1968; Jackson, 1972). These studies will not be considered further in this chapter. Instead, studies that have examined self-observation as the major independent variable will be emphasized. With the above points in mind we turn to a consideration of some recent self-observation studies.

McFall (1970) conducted a study to evaluate the effects of self-monitoring on smoking behavior. Sixteen college students who were regular smokers participated; in addition, sixteen nonsmokers served as observers. The situation involved a summer session course in abnormal psychology that met daily for 50 minutes. Nonsmokers were asked to observe the daily smoking behavior of the "smoking" student (S) who had been assigned the seat directly next to them. For nine consecutive class days the observer simply recorded the frequency of cigarettes smoked. The teacher then announced that he wanted to enlist the class's cooperation in collecting some data on the topic of smoking. He asked half of the smokers to keep a daily tally of the number of cigarettes they smoked during class. The other half were asked to record each time they had the desire (urge) to smoke but decided not to do so. Nonsmoking observers were instructed to continue collecting data on their smoking partners. The instructor, McFall, asked students not to make any changes in their normal smoking behavior since the whole idea of the experiment was to gather information on smokers under natural or typical circumstances. The self-observation lasted for thirteen consecutive class days. At the end of that time the teacher collected the data from all of the students and asked them to stop recording smoking behavior. A third phase then took place for eight consecutive days, during which time the observers continued to record the smoking behavior of their seating partner, supposedly without the individual's knowledge.

Figure 3–4 presents the results in terms of the smoking frequency of subjects who observed their actual smoking (smoke group) and those who recorded the frequency of their decisions not to smoke (no-smoke group). Although the average smoking rates for the six subjects in each group were practically identical during the first baseline period, statistically significant differences were found during the self-monitoring phase. The smoking group actually increased their smoking rate to 1.4, while the no-smoking group decreased their rate to approximately .06. This difference was maintained during the second baseline period in which both groups increased slightly. Again the difference between groups was significant ($p < .05$).

In terms of the reliability of self-observation, an overall correlation of .61 was found for the six smoker–observer pairs. When each of the six smoker–observer pairs was considered separately the correlation ranged between —.05 and 1.00; three of the six pairs were above .75. In general, the observer's estimate was less than the smoker's report of number of cigarettes smoked.

This study unfortunately suffers from several methodological problems (Kanfer, 1970a; Orne, 1970). Smokers and nonsmokers (i.e., those reporting their urge to smoke and decision not to smoke) may have known

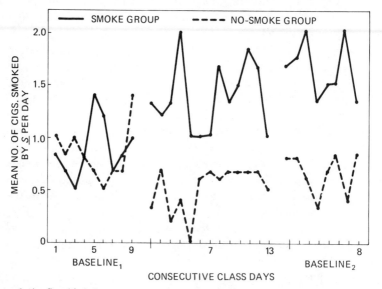

Figure 3–4 Smoking frequency across consecutive class days for two conditions of self-monitoring. (Adapted from R. M. McFall, "The Effects of Self-Monitoring on Normal Smoking Behavior," *Journal of Consulting and Clinical Psychology*, 1970, *35*, 139. Copyright 1970 by the American Psychological Association. Reprinted by permission.)

that they were being observed by classmates; such knowledge might have influenced their smoking behavior. Further, the investigator deliberately modeled smoking behavior during the first minute of class starting on the third day because "the smoking rate among smokers had been rather low." Such modeling may have explained in part the reason for the increase in smoking during the self-monitoring phase. More importantly, the question of reactivity (i.e., did self-observation of smoking influence smoking) was not clearly answered. Smokers were arbitrarily designated as experimental subjects, some of whom may have wanted to decrease their smoking and others who had no such interest. This combination of subjects makes interpretation of self-observation's reactivity difficult. Would subjects not motivated to reduce their smoking have increased their smoking during the self-observation phase when the experimenter was modeling smoking behavior?

This study did provide suggestive data that the timing and form of self-observation may be crucial. Given the limitations discussed above, the results suggest that observing an antecedent of the behavior in question (the urge to smoke) may be a more effective self-change strategy than observing a behavior after it has occurred. Moreover, for those students who did want to reduce their smoking, the self-recording of a desired response (CR+) that is, not smoking, may have been more effective than the self-monitoring of its less desired alternative (CR—), that is, smoking.

In a subsequent study Gottman and McFall (1972) examined self-observation effects on the classroom participation of seventeen high school sophomores in a special education class. After eight weeks (forty days) of baseline, during which a trained observer recorded the number of times each subject talked, eight students were asked to self-record each time they talked, while the other nine recorded each time they had an urge to talk but did not. After five days the students switched to the other type of self-observation for another five days. A follow-up phase then took place, during which self-observation was discontinued. The results indicated that self-observation of talking significantly influenced the frequency of talking only for the group that first observed their urges to talk. When talking was monitored before urges to talk, the frequency of talking during the latter phase was reduced. The sharp increase in talking displayed by the group that first observed urges was not maintained during the follow-up phase. This finding suggests that talking was under the control of self-observation during those five days since the mean frequency dropped sharply during the follow-up.

One of the problems in interpreting this study concerns the classroom teacher, who was clearly aware of which student was participating in which treatment—they had red and green cards given them by the teacher and kept on their desks. Since the teacher's behavior was not observed, there is no way of knowing if the dramatic increases for the urge-talk group were related to any selective attention or social approval by the teacher. The frequency of student participation is clearly subject to consequences provided by the teacher. Conceivably the teacher may have provided more social reinforcement during the second five-day phase, thereby increasing the participation for students self-observing participation (rather than urges to participate). The use of red and green cards readily cued the teacher as to which behavior each student was observing. It is also unclear from the study as to how knowledgeable the teacher was about the project in terms of the questions under study.

A commendable feature of the Gottman and McFall study was the use of an extended baseline period. Seldom is data provided that clearly establishes the stability and hence the reliability of the behavior *before* an intervention is used. In using an intensive time series design, these authors were able to establish the "naturalistic" frequency of the behavior under investigation before self-observation was started.

One of the most impressive existing studies on self-observation was reported by Broden, Hall, and Mitts (1971). These authors examined the effects of self-monitoring using an $N=1$ intensive design. The first experiment dealt with an eighth-grade girl named Lisa, who was concerned about doing very poorly in her history class. She had requested help from the school counselor, who, in conjunction with Lisa's teacher, made arrangements for an external observer to record the frequency of Lisa's studying behavior for a seven-day period. Starting on the eighth day Lisa was asked by the counselor to use a self-recording sheet and to indicate every few minutes with a plus or a minus whether she had been studying. Studying was defined as attending to a teacher-assigned task, facing the teacher, writing down lecture notes, facing a child who was responding to a teacher's question, or reciting when called upon by the teacher. "Nonstudy" behaviors included being out of her seat without permission, talking out without being recognized by the teacher, facing the window, fingering nonacademic objects such as her makeup, comb, or purse, or working on an assignment for another class. The external observer who remained in the classroom every day throughout the study also recorded the frequency of teacher attention to Lisa whenever it occurred.

Figure 3–5 presents the phases of this experiment indicating the percent of time Lisa engaged in studying during each phase of the study. During the baseline phase, Lisa's average rate of studying was about 30 percent, despite two conferences with her counselor and promises to try harder. When self-observation was initiated on the eighth day a significant increase was immediately produced with studying averaging about 80 percent. On the fourteenth day Lisa was told by the counselor that recording slips were not available, and the amount of study time promptly dropped to an average of about 27 percent for the next four days. When self-observation was reintroduced, study behavior again increased to an

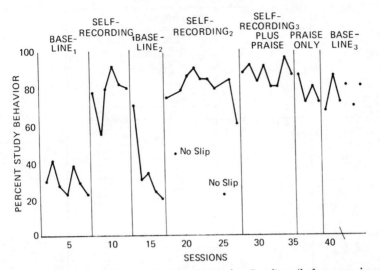

Figure 3–5   A record of Lisa's study behavior during *Baseline₁* (before experimental procedures); *Self-Recording₁* (Lisa recorded study or nonstudy on slips provided by counselor); *Baseline₂* (self-recording slips were withdrawn); *Self-Recording₂* (self-recording slips were reinstated); *Self-Recording₃ plus Praise* (self-recording slips were continued, and teacher praise for study increased); *Praise Only* (increased teacher praise was maintained, and self-recording withdrawn); and *Baseline₃* (teacher praise was decreased to baseline levels). (Adapted from M. Broden, R. V. Hall, & B. Mitts, "The Effect of Self-Recording on the Classroom Behavior of Two Eighth-Grade Students," *Journal of Applied Behavior Analysis*, 1971, 194. Copyright 1971 by the Society for the Experimental Analysis of Behavior, Inc.)

average of 80 percent. On two days self-observation was discontinued to examine if self-observation itself was maintaining the increase in study time. These "probes" (Sidman, 1960), indicated as "no slip" in Figure 3–5, showed that studying declined to 42 percent and 22 percent on these two days.

On the thirtieth day the teacher was asked to provide Lisa with attention and approval for her study behavior. During this final intervention the self-monitoring procedure was discontinued again, and the teacher was asked to continue using attention for Lisa's studying behavior. This resulted in a slight reduction in performance. In the final baseline phase the teacher was asked to discontinue any special attention to Lisa, and self-monitoring was also not used. Lisa's studying behavior averaged about 70 percent, well above the rate for the initial baseline period.

This study also provides valuable information on the reliability of self-observation. Although there was low agreement between Lisa's and the observer's estimates of the percent of time spent studying on a day-to-day basis—the variations ranged as high as 29 percent—the means for overall agreement for each phase were extremely similar. Figure 3–6

EXPERIMENTAL PHASE	OBSERVER	LISA
	78%	80%
	54%	70%
	79%	
SELF-RECORDING₁	92%	63%
	82%	79%
	80%	90%
MEAN	78%	76%
	75%	60%
	PROBE A	
	78%	100%
	87%	80%
	90%	Forgot
SELF-RECORDING₂	84%	Forgot
	84%	Forgot
	79%	75%
	PROBE B	
	83%	90%
	59%	Forgot
MEAN	80%	81%
	89%	Forgot
	93%	Forgot
	83%	Forgot
	92%	Forgot
SELF-RECORDING₃ PLUS PRAISE	81%	66%
	81%	100%
	96%	Forgot
	88%	100%
MEAN	88%	89%

Figure 3–6   A record of percent of study recorded by the observer and by Lisa during self-recording phases. (Adapted from M. Broden, R. V. Hall, & B. Mitts, "The Effect of Self-Recording on the Classroom Behavior of Two Eighth-Grade Students," *Journal of Applied Behavior Analysis*, 1971, 195. Copyright 1971 by the Society for the Experimental Analysis of Behavior, Inc.)

presents the record of the percent of time recorded by the observer and by Lisa during the self-monitoring phases of the study. Note that the day-to-day comparisons vary widely in some cases and that the mean comparisons for each phase are almost identical.

On four out of nine days during the second self-observation phase and on five out of eight days of the final self-observation phase Lisa failed to fill out her self-recording sheet. Despite this, Lisa's study behavior remained at a high level as indicated by the observer's data. These data suggest that the self-observation had acquired the power of a discriminative stimulus (S^d) or cue that prompted Lisa to engage in the behavior *without* necessarily counting the behavior. Lisa's studying behavior was apparently under the control of the recording slip even though she was not making use of it during class time. Recall that studying dropped to 42 percent and 22 percent on the days when Lisa was not given a self-recording sheet. An implication is that self-observation devices may themselves be used as discriminative cues to prompt and maintain self-controlling behaviors.

Another finding of interest concerns the unreliability of Lisa's daily data and yet the reliability of behavior change. Clearly there was limited agreement between Lisa's daily estimates of her study behavior and those reported by an independent observer. However, it was apparently not necessary for Lisa to provide highly reliable self-observation data in order to change. This issue relates to the general problem of reliability in self-observation data and the reliability of self-observation effects. The data from this study suggest that stable self-change can occur with fairly unreliable self-observations. The question is, of course, how unreliable can self-observations be and still effect desired changes.

Broden, Hall, and Mitts (1971) reported a second experiment that relates to the reactive or "therapeutic" effects of self-observation. An eighth-grade boy, Stu, had been referred for treatment due to his excessive talking out in class. Figure 3–7 presents the phases and the data for Stu's self-observation. Session A represents a 25-minute period before

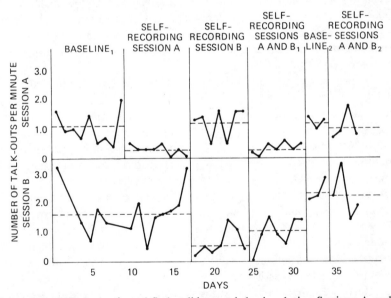

Figure 3–7   Self-observation of Stu's talking-out behavior during Sessions A and B of math class: *Baseline₁* (before experimental procedures); *Self-Recording, Session A* (Stu recorded his talk-outs during Session A only); *Self-Recording, Session B* (Stu recorded his talk-outs during Session B only); *Self-Recording, Sessions A and B₁* (Stu recorded his talk-outs during both math class sessions); *Baseline₂* (return to baseline conditions; self-recording slips were withdrawn); *Self-Recording, Sessions A and B₂* (Stu recorded his talk-outs for both A and B sessions). (Adapted from M. Broden, R. V. Hall, & B. Mitts, "The Effect of Self-Recording on the Classroom Behavior of Two Eighth-Grade Students," *Journal of Applied Behavior Analysis*, 1971, 197. Copyright 1971 by the Society for the Experimental Analysis of Behavior, Inc.)

lunch; Session B was comprised of a 20-minute interval after lunch. This multiple-baseline study found that Stu's self-observation reduced talking out only during the time period when self-observation occurred. Note that Stu's talking out decreased from more than one time per minute to about 0.3 times a minute during Session A; talking out actually increased during Session B for the same time period. Also note that during Session B, talking out during Session A quickly returned to its baseline level. Finally, Figure 3–7 clearly illustrates that the effects of self-observation were temporary. In the final phase, when Stu was self-recording for both sessions, talking out had returned to the original baseline level for Session A and had *increased* slightly during Session B. Unfortunately the data for the final phase were unstable. With four highly variable data points, conclusions about direction and level of the behavior must remain very limited (Thoresen, in press).

Several points are important in contrasting the results of self-observation for Lisa and Stu. First, Lisa had requested help in improving her grades. Her counselor had suggested that self-observation might be a way of helping her with her problem. Hence Lisa was highly motivated to change and was given the expectancy that self-observation would be helpful. Stu, by contrast, had not requested help, nor was he given any individual attention from his teacher or counselor about his problem of talking out excessively.

Second, the effects of self-observation on Lisa are confounded by the weekly conferences with her counselor; during these conferences the counselor reviewed her progress and deliberately praised her for any improvement. Stu received no such attention for improvement from his classroom teacher or anyone else. Stu's performance illustrates an important point in self-control procedures: The external environment must at some point provide differential reinforcement for the behavior being changed. Otherwise the effects of self-observation (as well as any other individual self-change technique) will probably have a short-lived effect.

Further support for the reactive effects of self-monitoring was reported by Mahoney, Moore, Wade, and Moura (1973), who investigated the relative effects of continuous versus intermittent self-observation. College students were offered assistance in their review preparation for the Graduate Record Examination. A linear teaching machine was programmed with appropriate review problems. Control subjects did not receive feedback on the accuracy of their review answers and were not instructed to self-monitor their performance. A second control group was provided with accuracy feedback but was likewise uninformed about self-recording. Two formal self-monitoring groups were employed. For these subjects, a small counter was attached to the teaching machine, and they were instructed to activate the counter either after every correct response (continuous self-monitoring) or after every third correct response (intermittent self-monitoring). An analysis of the amount of time spent reviewing problems showed that subjects in both self-monitoring conditions remained for significantly longer lengths of time than did control subjects. This effect was more pronounced for individuals who recorded every correct answer (continuous). Moreover, self-monitoring subjects showed progressively superior accuracy on quantitative problems. An unobtrusive reliability check revealed that self-monitoring subjects were very consistent in their recording ($r=.94$). These findings suggest that the effects of self-monitoring may not reflect simple secondary reinforcement processes. However, further research on the frequency and scheduling of self-observation is needed.

In a comparative group design, Johnson and White (1971) investigated the effect of self-observation on college students' study time over a period of several weeks. Three groups were involved: a self-observation of study behavior group, a self-observation of dating behavior group (as control for the nonspecific effects of self-observation), and a no-contact control group, who were simply informed that more people had volunteered than had been anticipated. Students in the self-observation group were provided with a packet of preaddressed postcards, each containing a printed form for daily recording. They were also given graph paper for their daily and weekly data, and directions on how to self-observe. To facilitate the observation of study behavior, a point system for study output was devised so that each study activity was appropriately rated. Points were given for such things as reading a text and studying notes for a quiz; for example, each page of assigned reading was worth three points. Subjects were instructed to sum their point total daily and to enter this total in the appropriate place on the postcard and graph paper. They were also told to sum their weekly points and graph this data. Postcards were returned each week to the experimenter, either in class or by mail. Subjects in the self-observation of dating group were given the same instructions except that they were asked to record the time spent in dating activities (defined as any recreational activity involving the opposite sex).

The effects of self-observation were evaluated by analyzing changes in weekly course grades. Analyses revealed that the study group received significantly higher grades on the average than the control group over a period of ten weeks. However, the differences between the study group and dating group were not significant. The authors suggest that one explanation for this might have been that students self-monitoring their dating behavior became more aware of the time spent in dating and possibly the time they should spend in studying. They may have increased their studying time. However, no data are presented for this conjecture.

This particular study highlights some of the methodological problems that must be addressed in self-observation research (e.g., control of extraneous influences and the use of appropriate designs). For example, students in this study were penalized for terminating the experiment. Our present understanding of self-observation phenomena necessitates the use of well-controlled designs that allow the investigator to maximize experimental control and, at the same time, gather detailed data on performances over time.

McFall and Hammen (1971) studied four kinds of self-observation procedures for the reduction of smoking behavior. In the "self-monitoring" group, subjects were simply told to keep daily records of their cigarette consumption. In a second group, called the *negative self-monitoring* group, subjects were provided with a wrist counter on which they were to record a negative point each time they were unable to resist smoking a cigarette. As they recorded a point they were also to subvocalize "I do not want to smoke." *Positive self-monitoring* constituted a third group. In this treatment subjects used a wrist counter each time they successfully resisted the temptation to smoke; they also subvocalized "I do not want to smoke." The fourth group, termed a *fixed-positive self-monitoring* group, was identical with the positive self-monitoring group with this exception: Each person was required to earn at least twenty positive points on his wrist counter each day. If in the course of each day they had experienced a decreased temptation to smoke and, therefore, could not earn the required twenty points, they were to "conjure up the desire, resist it, and record a point"; that is, they were to imagine themselves wanting a cigarette and then not have one.

All subjects met in an initial group setting and were instructed to stop smoking "cold turkey." They were given smoking record sheets to be handed in twice weekly for three weeks and were asked to buy all cigarettes at the Smoking Clinic. Following the initial group meeting each subject visited the clinic twice a week to hand in his smoking record, to obtain a new record form and to buy more cigarettes if necessary. According to the authors all subjects engaged in self-observation, the only difference being that each group received different kinds of self-observation instructions. Consistent with a host of previous smoking reduction studies, these authors found no significant differences among the four self-monitoring treatments. The negative and fixed-positive groups had slightly more subjects who achieved total abstinence from smoking, but the differences were very small.

This study was designated as an examination of the nonspecific factors in smoking reduction through self-monitoring. However, the treatments described above point out a major problem in self-observation studies, namely, a confounding of self-observation with other kinds of overt and covert self-change techniques. For example, it is clear that the negative and positive self-monitoring treatments in this study involved not only observing and recording data, but also evaluative self-reinforcement and self-punishment. The fixed-positive self-monitoring group likewise used imagery in addition to simple self-recording. Clearly the four groups were not all using the same self-observation treatment.

This study again illustrates the need for experimental designs that examine self-observation in a more controlled manner. The act of self-recording must be conceptualized in terms of more specific operations and not confused with other kinds of self-change techniques, such as the use of subvocalizations and the assigning of evaluative points contingent upon performance. While such procedures may, of course, enhance the therapeutic effect of a treatment program, they obscure our understanding of self-observation processes.

An interesting study of the effects of self-observation is presented by Kunzelmann (1970) in the case of a 7-year-old student, Kim, who engaged in a considerable amount of classroom whining behavior. The teacher decided to observe the frequency of whining over a period of thirty days, during which she found that the child whined about 2½ times every hour. Using the countoon procedure described earlier (see Figure 3–3), the child was instructed to record the frequency on his countoon chart each time whining occurred. Figure 3–8 presents the results of self-observation on a semilogarithmic chart. A reduction was clearly demon-

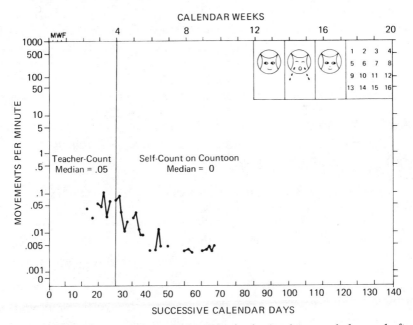

Figure 3–8   Frequency of Kim's whining behavior in the classroom before and after self-observation. (Teacher counted whining during baseline.) (Adapted from H. Kunzelmann (Ed.), *Precision Teaching*, Seattle, Wash.: Special Child Publications, 1970, 108. Reproduced with permission.)

strated as soon as the self-observation procedure was introduced. After approximately ten days, whining behavior had been completely eliminated, a change maintained for 6 weeks.

Kunzelmann (1970) also reports another self-observation study involving weight loss in which he was the subject. The frequency of bites of food was selected as the behavior to be controlled on the assumption that it relates directly to weight loss and weight gain. Kunzelmann initially found that 184 bites of food were being consumed daily. This intake was maintaining a body weight of 250 pounds. After seven days of recording, a decision was made to reduce bite frequency as a way of reducing body weight. No other action was taken. Self-observation continued over thirteen weeks during which time over 31 pounds were lost in a steady decelerating rate of a little over two pounds per week. A threefold reduction in bites per day was achieved and maintained for the thirteen-week period.

In an ingenious study, Thomas, Abrams, and Johnson (1971) used self-observation along with systematic desensitization to reduce multiple tics in an 18-year-old male. These tics consisted of "involuntary" vocal noises (a barklike sound and hissing noises) and a jerking movement of the neck. To help determine what environmental conditions might be controlling these behaviors, an elaborate system for observing the patient in various settings was employed (e.g., the drugstore, church, restaurant, and library). The patient was provided with a mechanical counter and asked to count *all* noises related to the vocal tic. During the first day he was to check the counter every fifteen minutes and report his count to an observer who was following him. After reporting the frequency he reset the counter and resumed recording. The patient was given brief practice in how to use the counter unobtrusively. The same procedure was followed on the second day except that the observer was not present at all times. Self-observation of minor vocal sounds and the neck tic was conducted in a similar fashion. Systematic desensitization (see Chapter 6) and drugs were also used in their treatment.

The effects of these treatment procedures were dramatic. In one day the rate of the vocal tic was reduced from more than four per minute (over 400 on Day 1) to essentially zero. Self-monitoring was continued for 12 days with no appreciable relapse either in the hospital or in community settings. A gradual reduction in minor vocal sounds and neck tics was likewise reported. Interpretation of this study is unfortunately confounded by the combination of several treatment strategies. In addition to the possible influence of desensitization and drugs, social reinforcement was employed—on Day 2 the observer "commended" the patient whenever he reported a bark rate of less than .5 per minute. The study does, however, provide a useful illustration of explicit, graduated training in self-observation. Furthermore, the data do support the notion that self-monitoring procedures were partially responsible for the reduction.

Leitenberg, Agras, Thompson, and Wright (1968) reported an experimental case study of a 51-year-old hospitalized claustrophobic woman, who was given a counting device (a stop watch) and asked to observe and record her behavior—the number of seconds spent in a closed room. Using an ABA design, self-monitoring was found to be effective in increasing the amount of time spent in the room. Improvement was reportedly maintained for 3 months, at which time the subject was discharged from the hospital.

Few researchers have attempted to isolate the components of conventional self-monitoring procedures. In a study reported by McNamara (1972), subjects volunteered for a program dealing with nail biting. In one condition, individuals were told to record actual instances of nail biting, whereas other subjects were instructed to record other incompatible behaviors (e.g., finger tapping, pulling hand away from mouth). Noteworthy in this study is the inclusion of a group that did not engage in any kind of self-observation. All groups demonstrated a significant increase in nail length during the four-week study. These findings suggest that demand characteristics and expectancy effects may account for much of the reactivity attributed to self-monitoring.

Recently Mahoney, Moura, and Wade (1973) compared the effectiveness of self-observation procedures with self-reward and self-punishment techniques in the modification of eating behavior. All subjects were given a small booklet describing stimulus-control strategies for reducing eating behavior. Subjects in the experimental groups were asked to weigh themselves twice weekly and to record their weight as well as their eating habits. An information control group was included in which subjects received the same booklets but did not participate in any self-observation. Compared with the self-reward and self-punishment groups, individuals who only self-monitored during this study demonstrated the *least* amount of weight loss. They were no more successful than information control subjects. These results lend support to the notion that, to be effective, self-observation procedures must be supplemented with other treatment strategies.

In a subsequent weight reduction study using 49 subjects, Mahoney (in press) compared a self-observation treatment with two types of self-reinforcement procedures (see Chapter 4). A modified time-sampling recording system was employed. Subjects in all groups demonstrated dramatic initial weight losses during a two-week baseline in which they self-monitored body weight and eating habits. However, despite the addition of weekly goals, the self-observation treatment failed to effect continued weight reduction. In this study, self-monitoring had a dramatic but short-lived effect on behavior, and wide individual variations were reported. In subjects for whom self-observation procedures were not supplemented by other motivational strategies (e.g., self-reward), the initial rate of progress

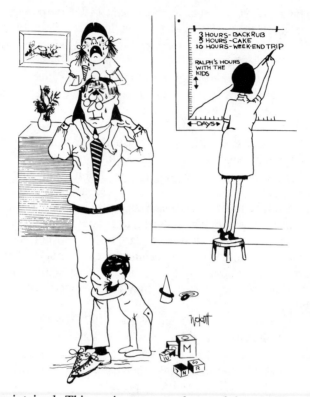

was not maintained. This again suggests the need for auxiliary treatment methods for the long-term self-management of effortful behavior.

Self-observation procedures have also been used in the modification of covert behaviors. For example, a study reported by Rutner and Bugle (1969) described the case of a hospitalized schizophrenic patient who reported hearing voices that controlled her behavior. She was asked to record and chart the frequency of her hallucinations. After the third day of self-observation, the patient's chart was posted on the hospital ward. Public display of this data understandably brought comment from the patients and staff. The reported hallucinations decreased from an initial level of 91 to zero after the first experimental day. After increasing to 60 on the next day, the frequency again declined to zero, with no further hallucinations reported over a period of 3 months. The authors suggest that posting the frequency chart on the ward changed the patient's hallucinations from a private, unobservable event, impervious to the actions of others, to a public affair with the opportunity for social reinforcement and disapproval. Terrace (1971) and others have pointed out the functional immunities of private events. As long as the response is *only* observable to the person, there is little opportunity for environmental consequences to influence these behaviors.

The issue of establishing the reliability and validity of self-reports concerning covert events poses difficult methodological problems. Obviously, there is no way to confirm directly or independently whether the recorded frequency of positive self-thoughts, for example, actually took place. Overt correlates of covert events can, however, provide some corroboration (Mahoney, Thoresen, & Danaher, 1972).

SUMMARY

Self-observation as a complex pattern of behaviors represents something more than the vague awareness and insight of most psychodynamic orientations. As presented here, self-observation involves responses that are *not* the same as the behavior being observed. These responses first consist of a discrimination that is cued by either an overt or covert stimulus. Discrimination is followed by a recording of the behavior, this frequently transformed into graphs. Finally, the data undergo some type of analysis or evaluation in which the collected data are compared with implicit or explicit performance standards. This behavioral perspective of self-observation raises a host of questions that remain unanswered.

The existing data on self-monitoring suggest the following tentative generalizations:

1. Individuals are not "naturally" accurate self-observers. Training in the discrimination and recording of a behavior is essential. Such training may be enhanced by modeling, immediate accuracy feedback, systematic reinforcement, and graduated transfer of recording responsibilities (external to self).
2. The accuracy of self-recorded data varies dramatically across subjects, situations, behaviors, and recording systems. Discrete behaviors and simple recording systems appear to enhance self-monitoring accuracy.
3. As a measurement device, self-observation represents a crucial preliminary stage in successful self-regulation. The individual may need accurate data on both his own behavior and relevant controlling influences before an effective self-change program can be developed.
4. As a treatment technique, the effects of self-observation are often variable and short-lived. Unless supplemented by additional behavior change influences (e.g., social reinforcement), self-monitoring does not offer promise in the long-term maintenance of effortful behavior. Speculations about possible causes of wide individual differences in reaction to self-monitoring (e.g., covert self-reactions) remain to be researched.
5. The use of explicit goals may or may not enhance the effects of self-observation, depending on the nature of the behavior and the goals adopted. Controlled research is again lacking.

In addition to the above generalizations, several research issues face contemporary investigators in self-monitoring. Does the desirability of the targeted behavior influence self-monitoring effects, such as observing instances of smoking (undesirable) vs. not smoking when the urge to smoke occurs (desirable)? Although preliminary hypotheses have suggested that a self-monitored behavior will change in the direction of social desirability (i.e., self-recording will increase socially approved behaviors but decrease disapproved behaviors), the existing data are not clear-cut. Another research-worthy question is whether there are behaviors whose self-recording is contratherapeutic (e.g., suicidal thoughts). Finally, should self-observation be aimed at early or late elements in a response chain (e.g., erotic thoughts versus actual sexual performance)?

Self-monitoring provides a method by which a person can become quantifiably more aware of both his own behavior and the factors that influence it. As such it represents an important first step in the development and implementation of effective self-control techniques. Preliminary evidence suggests that self-observation functions both as a measurement and a preliminary self-change strategy. Further research on the processes and promise of systematic self-observation is sorely needed.

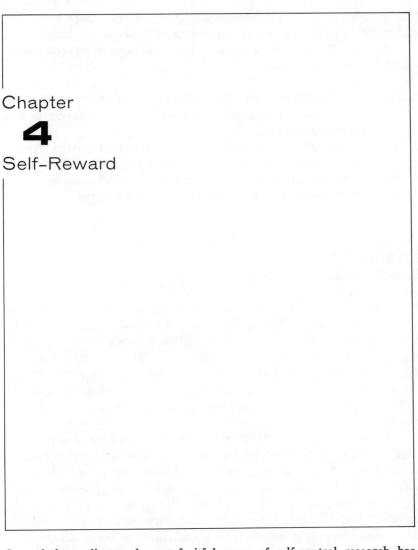

Chapter

4

Self-Reward

One of the earliest and most fruitful areas of self-control research has been self-reward. In Chapter 1 self-reward (or self-reinforcement) was categorized as to whether the person presents himself contingently with a positive stimulus (positive self-reward) or contingently removes some negative stimulus (negative self-reward). A mundane illustration of positive self-reward might be the housewife who awards herself a special purchase for having attained a personal goal. Negative self-reward is illustrated by the weight-watcher who places uncomplimentary pictures of herself on a bulletin board and then removes them one by one for having made weight loss progress.

Our discussion of self-reward will be divided into sections on laboratory research and clinical applications. Later in the chapter we will address some of the theoretical and conceptual issues in this area.

Among the questions that have been investigated by self-reward researchers are the following:

1. Does self-administered reinforcement have the same effects as externally controlled rewards? Can it strengthen and maintain behavior as well as external reinforcement?
2. Can the principles of external reinforcement (e.g., schedules, reward magnitude, etc.) be directly applied to self-reward?
3. What techniques are most effective in training an individual to reward his own performances? What factors influence the acquisition of self-reward?

SELF–REWARD:
LABORATORY RESEARCH

All of the existing laboratory studies dealing with self-reward have focused on the positive variety. The defining characteristic of positive self-reward is that the person has free access to a reinforcing behavior but engages in it only after having exhibited some performance (Skinner, 1953; Bandura, 1971b). A type of self-denial is, therefore, involved (Premack, 1972). Even though the industrious student *could* leave his desk at any moment and go to the ever-reinforcing refrigerator, he chooses not to do so until having completed a course assignment.

Kanfer (1970b) and Bandura (1971b) have both placed very heavy emphasis on the role of self-reinforcement (both tangible and symbolic) in many self-control patterns. Their conceptual approaches, which are very compatible, have focused on three separate components in self-regulatory patterns: (1) self-monitoring, (2) evaluative or comparison processes, and (3) self-reinforcement. The self-evaluation that occurs in the second component results from comparisons of one's self-observed performance to social or self-imposed performance standards. Subsequent self-presented consequences may be positive (self-reward) or negative (self-punishment) and may take a variety of forms (see Chapter 6 for a discussion of covert consequences).

The research efforts of Bandura, Kanfer, and their colleagues have been directed at the exploration of self-reward processes in laboratory settings. While sharing the same general conceptual approach, these workers have varied in both their experimental methodology and in the focus of their research. Kanfer and his colleagues have generally employed a *directed learning paradigm* (cf. Kanfer, 1970b) in which subjects initially are trained externally (using experimenter-administered reinforcements) and are subsequently asked to assume responsibility for presenting their own rewards. The *social learning paradigm* is one used predominantly by Bandura and his co-workers. In this strategy subjects initially observe an adult or peer model displaying self-reward procedures and are later placed in a situation where they have the option of rewarding themselves. Kanfer's research has generally dealt with college students, while Bandura's has dealt with young children. In addition to the above-described differences in the means by which experimental self-reward patterns are established, two other methodological differences can be noted: (1) the form of the self-presented reward, and (2) the type of performance task employed. Research by the Kanfer group has generally involved ambiguous verbal or perceptual learning tasks where the correctness of the subject's response is very difficult to ascertain. The rewarding stimulus in these experiments is often a symbolic one (e.g., a green light with the word "correct" written on it). On the other hand, the experiments by Bandura and his co-workers have usually involved discrete motoric responses (e.g., turning a hand crank, bowling) where explicit performance feedback is supplied. The tasks are usually chosen to minimize the possibility of previously experienced standards (cf. Bandura, 1971a). The rewarding stimulus in these experiments is generally candy or redeemable tokens. Thus these two research groups have taken different procedural approaches to the exploration of self-reward phenomena. Rather than alternate between these two paradigms in our discussion, we shall address ourselves separately to each.

Kanfer's Directed Learning Paradigm

Kanfer and his co-workers have investigated a variety of parameters bearing on the development, maintenance, and influence of experimental self-reward patterns. Their initial research was concerned with the amount of initial training given to subjects before they are asked to assume self-reward responsibilities (Kanfer, Bradley, & Marston, 1962). Evidence from several experiments revealed that degree of initial learning is positively correlated with appropriate self-reinforcement.

Subsequent research explored the effects of various training influences on acquisition of self-reward patterns. Using direct training procedures, Kanfer and Marston (1963a) found that lenient versus stringent instructions regarding subjects' standards of self-reinforcement resulted in correspondingly different rates of self-reward: Lenient instructions produced frequent and often inaccurate self-reward, while stringent instructions resulted in relatively infrequent self-reward. Pursuing these findings, Kanfer and Marston (1963b) varied social approval for self-reinforcement. During a training phase subjects were either encouraged or discouraged in their self-presentation of rewards (nonredeemable poker chips). Data from a subsequent test phase showed that individuals who had received social approval for their self-reward presented themselves with significantly more chips than subjects who had been discouraged.

The social aspects of self-reward training were further researched by Marston (1965), who used a variation of Bandura's social learning paradigm. After obtaining baseline rates of verbal self-praise for "popular" word associations, subjects listened to a tape recording in which a model verbally rewarded himself at either a high or low rate. Subsequent test trials showed that subjects' self-reward rates were dramatically affected by this modeling experience. Individuals who witnessed the highly self-rewarding model displayed significantly higher rates of subsequent self-reward than subjects who had listened to the less rewarding model. Moreover, they imposed these standards on another person whose performance they were asked to monitor. A partial replication of this study was reported by Marston and Smith (1968). As we shall see in the next section, these findings are very consistent with those reported by Bandura and his co-workers in their research on vicarious acquisition of self-control patterns.

The modifiability of self-reward rates was investigated by Marston (1969), who employed a pseudosubliminal perception task and self-awarded points (nonredeemable). After a baseline measurement of subjects' self-reward rates, they received positive feedback (praise) from the experimenter contingent upon either (1) having self-rewarded on that trial or (2) not having self-rewarded. The results indicated that self-reward rate was affected by subsequent external consequences, particularly when initial frequency of self-reinforcement was low. A paradoxical finding was that contingent positive feedback for *not* self-rewarding produced increases in initially low self-reward rates.

Rate of external reinforcement during initial training has also received experimental attention. In contrast to the above study, which manipulated the external consequences of self-rewarding responses, these inquiries have dealt with the training frequency of external reinforcement. If a subject is generously rewarded by an experimenter for his training performances, will he subsequently adopt generous (lenient) standards for his self-presentation of rewards? In a sense these standards represent reinforcement schedules. Will an individual employ a self-reward schedule that is similar to the external schedule on which he was trained? If so, does the principle of "intermittent" or "partial" reinforcement (Ferster & Skinner, 1957) apply to self-regulated reward systems? That is, can one expect better maintenance of a behavior if it is self-rewarded occasionally rather than after every occurrence?

The pioneering work in this area was performed by Kanfer (1964), who trained subjects on fixed reinforcement ratios for lever-pulling responses. After every tenth, twenty-fifth, or fiftieth response, subjects received a reinforcement (pennies); they were subsequently asked to reward themselves for their performance. Data analyses revealed that they self-rewarded at relatively stable rates, using ratios from approximately 30 percent to 50 percent of those experienced during training.

Another study dealing with the effects of intermittent training schedules was performed by Marston (1964a). Using a nonsense syllable discrimination task with a green light as the reward, ninety subjects were trained using reinforcement schedules of 100 percent (continuous), 75 percent, or 50 percent. He found that frequency of self-reward generally paralleled the previous training frequency of reinforcement. Subjects self-imposed roughly the same schedules on which they had been trained. Contrary to an intermittency generalization, subjects who adopted "leaner" (i.e., less frequent) schedules of self-reward displayed poorer accuracy.

Further support for the correspondence between self-imposed schedules and external (training) schedules has been reported (Kanfer & Duerfeldt, 1968b; Dorsey, Kanfer, & Duerfeldt, 1971). Moreover, there is some evidence that individuals are consistent across tasks in the self-reward standards that they adopt (Marston, 1964b; Kanfer, Duerfeldt, & LePage, 1969). An interesting finding in this latter study was that individual rates of self-reward were not related to rates of self-criticism. Contrary to a frequent clinical assumption, individuals who generously self-rewarded were not correspondingly less self-critical.

As indicated by the above studies, the effects of reinforcement schedules on self-reward acquisition have received only preliminary research. Of particular note is the absence of data regarding the differential maintenance effects of various schedules of self-reward. Related to this issue is the question of whether self-presented reinforcements (on any schedule) have the same effects as externally administered ones. In other words, does self-reward produce the same degree of behavior change or maintenance as external reward?

One of the earliest studies comparing the effects of external reward and self-reward was reported by Marston and Kanfer (1963), who trained sixty-two male undergraduates on a nonsense-syllable discrimination task. After reaching a 60 percent accuracy criterion, subjects were exposed to one of three conditions: (1) continued training (experimenter-administered reinforcement for correct responding), (2) extinction (cessation of reinforcement), or (3) self-reinforcement. Within groups the magnitude of the reinforcing stimulus was also varied (a green light, non-redeemable poker chips, or tokens redeemable for small prizes). Analyses revealed that subjects differed significantly in their accuracy during the test phase of the experiment. Individuals who received continued training improved their accuracy; self-reinforcement subjects maintained their accuracy at its previous level, and extinction subjects significantly declined. Level of incentive did not affect either accuracy or rate of self-rein-forcement. Subjects who were given the opportunity to award themselves redeemable chips, however, showed greater caution and conservatism in their self-reinforcement.

Findings somewhat contradictory to these were reported by Marston (1967) in a study evaluating the relative effects of external reinforcement, self-reinforcement, and accuracy feedback on subjects' dart-throwing skills and line-length estimation. The results of this study suggested a slight inferiority of external reinforcement with near equivalence of self-reward and feedback-only procedures.

Two studies by Kanfer and Duerfeldt also investigated the relative effects of external reinforcement and self-reinforcement. In the first (1967b), subjects who received no information on their performance accuracy showed recall and relearning scores on a nonsense-syllable task superior to subjects in either a self-reward or external reward condition. The second study (1967c) used a geometric match-to-sample task and random (noncontingent) external reinforcement. In a subsequent test phase, subjects who had been given the opportunity to reward their own performances performed better than subjects in control, extinction, and external reward groups. Self-reward subjects closely matched their training schedules and, in spite of the random and uninformative nature of their previous reinforcement, displayed an impressive consistency (77.5 per-cent) in rewarding themselves only on correct trials. The noncontingent nature of initial training reinforcements in this study unfortunately com-plicates its interpretation.

Johnson (1970) explored the relative effects of external and self-reinforcement in the maintenance of attentive behavior on the part of first- and second-grade children. Using a match-to-sample discrimination task, subjects were given a baseline assessment and then externally trained with points redeemable for candy and toys. In the next phase, two groups of subjects continued on external reward and a third was given training in self-reward. In the latter group, incorrect self-presentations of points were not backed up by candy and toys. A test phase was then introduced. One of the external reward groups continued receiving experi-menter-administered points and the second group entered extinction (termination of reinforcement was announced). The children who had received self-reward training were told to present themselves with points after correct responses. The experimenter remained in the room with external reward and extinction subjects but was absent in the self-reward condition. Since this was a test phase, incorrect self-rewards were backed up by candy and toy prizes. Then came a reversal to baseline conditions (termination of all rewards), followed by a retraining phase and then a transfer test. The results showed that children receiving external and self-reinforcement performed better than children who experienced the extinction condition. An initial superiority of self-reward over external reward was evidenced at the beginning of their extinction phase (second baseline). No transfer differences were found. These findings are unfortunately confounded by the varying presence of the experimenter in the different conditions and the fact that extinction was announced in one group. However, as will be seen in the next section, they are consistent with other research reporting the equivalent maintaining capabilities of both external and self-reward systems.

Again using match-to-sample problems and points redeemable for prizes, Johnson and Martin (in press) trained sixty children using external reinforcement. Subjects were then divided into three groups: (1) external reinforcement, (2) self-reinforcement, and (3) noncontingent reinforcement (control). Prizes awarded to children in the latter condition were presented as being unrelated to their performance accuracy. Points were awarded by the experimenter in the external and noncontingent groups. For self-reward subjects, the evaluative verbalization "I was right" produced points. Subsequently, the schedule of reinforcement in all three groups was progressively thinned. External and noncontingent reward subjects began receiving points only after their second, third, and fifth correct responses. For self-reward children, points were awarded only after their second, third, and fifth "I was right" verbalizations. An extinction period followed in which external reinforcement and self-reinforcement subjects received initial reinforcement for every fifth correct or "I was right" response (respectively) and then experienced fifteen minutes of nonreward. The data indicated that the noncontingent reward group was inferior to the other two, which did not differ from one another. Self-reward subjects, however, did display some superiority over external reward children during initial extinction and in the presence of one of the intermittent schedules (a fixed ratio of 3).

These findings are unfortunately confounded by some rather serious methodological problems. For example, unlike the other groups, noncontingent reward subjects did not receive any initial reinforcement at the beginning of extinction. External reward subjects were also not instructed to verbalize "I was right" after correct responses as were children in the other two groups. Finally, and perhaps most seriously, the scheduling of reinforcement was *external* for self-reward subjects. In this condition every second, third, or fifth "I was right" response—regardless of its accuracy—did produce points, but control over those points was obviously in the hands of the experimenter and not the subject. This procedure amounted to the intermittent external reinforcement of positive self-evaluative statements. While the latter constitutes an interesting research study, it was not the purpose of the reported research. The findings of this study do, however, have important implications for the significance of learned self-evaluative patterns. As we shall see in Chapter 6, covert self-evaluations may often be the unsung heroes in the persistence of many a self-regulatory endeavor.

In an experiment that employed instructions rather than training, Montgomery and Parton (1970) gave elementary school children an ambiguous matching task and told them to pull a lever if they thought they had been correct. For half of the subjects, the lever pull produced a penny (subjects, however, were not allowed to keep the penny); this procedure was labeled self-reinforcement. The results of this study showed that the children tended to repeat previously self-rewarded responses more frequently than nonrewarded ones. These findings were interpreted as supporting the reinforcing effects of self-presented rewards.

The above research has suggested some variability in the behavior change and maintenance potential of self-reward, particularly within the ambiguous task and symbolic reward format of the directed learning paradigm. However, as will be seen in the next section, evidence from other laboratory paradigms and applied clinical research offers support for the notion that systematic self-reward can provide a powerful behavior change influence.

Before leaving the directed learning research of Kanfer and his colleagues, mention should be made of their explorations (e.g., Marston, 1964c) into the role of personality variables in self-reward. For example, two studies (Kanfer, 1966; Kanfer & Duerfeldt, 1968a) involving more than 1500 elementary students evaluated the relationship between unmerited self-reward (cheating) and such variables as age, class standing, and so on. In both studies, there was a dramatic decline in cheating as age and class standing increased. Findings such as these again suggest that socialization processes play a very important role in the acquisition and maintenance of self-regulatory patterns (Kohlberg, 1969). Moreover, the finding that academically successful students showed more restraint and consistency in their self-administration of rewards suggests the possible need for early self-management training in educational systems (Glaser, 1972; Thoresen & Hosford, 1973).

It would be difficult to capsulize the significance and implications of the foregoing research by Kanfer, Marston, and their colleagues. A partial summary is provided in Kanfer's (1970b) excellent review of the area. Briefly, and within the ambiguous task and symbolic self-reward paradigm employed by these workers, the following generalizations seem warranted:

1. Self-reward training may enhance an individual's maintenance of a response; this maintenance is somewhat variable with respect to that evidenced after external reward training.
2. Rate and standard of self-reinforcement are influenced by leniency instructions, modeled standards, and social reinforcement.

3. Self-reward rates tend to parallel previous (training) rates of external reinforcement.
4. Self-reward rates tend to be stable within brief testing situations and show some degree of consistency across tasks.
5. There appears to be at least partial independence between verbal self-evaluation and actual self-reinforcement; self-reward and self-criticism seem to be independent of one another.
6. Self-reward rates are affected by training schedules and by the individual's competence at the target task.
7. As the ambiguity of the task or performance standard increases, the rate of self-reward declines.
8. As the magnitude of the rewarding stimulus increases, the individual becomes more conservative in his self-reward.
9. Lack of adherence to prescribed self-reward standards appears to correlate inversely with age and with certain intellectual or achievement variables.

As with any laboratory analogue, there are possible problems of generalization and relevance to actual field applications. For example, the use of a green light as the sole rewarding stimulus in much of the Kanfer *et al.* research might be criticized due to its remoteness to clinically useful self-reinforcements. The use of ambiguous laboratory tasks has also been cited as a methodological contamination (Bandura, 1971b) due to the subsequent interaction of self-evaluative and self-reinforcement processes. In the directed learning paradigm employed by Kanfer, it is quite possible for a subject to evaluate his response as being correct without judging it worthy of self-reward. Kanfer (1970b) defends task ambiguity as simulating naturalistic self-reward situations wherein the target response may consist of a developing skill. However, there can be little doubt that the laboratory paradigm has often been far removed from clinical problems.

Despite the possible deficiencies of the directed learning paradigm, the research by Kanfer, Marston, and their colleagues has added tremendously to our understanding of self-reinforcement processes. The relevance and validity of their findings has been best supported by derivative clinical applications, which are discussed in a later section. Moreover, the theoretical framework that has developed as a result of directed learning research has been invaluable in the interpretation and understanding of many self-regulatory phenomena (Kanfer & Phillips, 1970; Kanfer, 1970b, 1971; Kanfer & Karoly, 1972b).

Bandura's Social Learning Paradigm

As discussed earlier the research reported by Bandura and his colleagues has differed both operationally and focally from that of the Kanfer group. Most of the investigations of Bandura *et al.* have been aimed at understanding the role of modeling processes in the transmission of self-reward patterns. In these studies, the target response has usually been a discrete motor response, and the self-presented reward has been tangible.

The earliest research in this paradigm was reported by Bandura and Kupers (1964), who investigated the effects of different modeling performances on children's subsequent adoption of self-reward standards. The apparatus employed was a miniature bowling game that was designed to allow the experimenters to control unobtrusively (and therefore standardize) individual performance feedback. Elementary school children observed either an adult or a peer model playing the game, verbalizing performance self-evaluations, and occasionally rewarding himself with candy. The modeled self-reward standards were systematically varied so that half the subjects in each condition observed minimal performances being self-rewarded, while the other half observed a model who rewarded himself only after high performance scores. Children in a control condition did not observe a model. All subjects were subsequently invited to play the game and to treat themselves to candy. The results showed that subjects exposed to the low-standard model rewarded themselves more frequently than subjects exposed to the high-standard model. The latter consistently imposed stringent performance standards on themselves. Control subjects were generally indiscriminate in their self-reward and showed no consistent relationship between performance score and the amount of candy taken. The adult models were slightly more effective than peer models in transmitting differential self-reward standards. Interestingly, 27 percent of the experimental subjects exactly reproduced the verbal self-evaluations of their models.

In a partial replication of the above findings, Bandura and Whalen (1966) exposed children to (1) a very competent model who received high performance scores and imposed stringent self-reward standards, (2) a moderately competent model who received and self-rewarded midrange scores, (3) an incompetent model who obtained low scores and was very lenient in his self-reinforcement, or (4) no model. The bowling game task was employed and candy again served as the rewarding stimulus. Subjects' standardized performance scores were approximately those of the moderately competent model. Data analyses again revealed that children's standards of self-reward were significantly affected by their previous exposure to modeling. Subjects who observed the moderate and high competence models were more stringent in their adopted self-reward standards. Control subjects again showed no selectivity in their reward of varying performances. Interestingly, those children who were exposed to the highly competent model rejected or at least compromised the model's rigorous standards and adopted more moderate performance criteria. This finding was interpreted as being consistent with social comparison theory, which states that an individual will be less likely to adopt modeled values or standards if the skills of the model are markedly discrepant from his own. Colle and Bee (1968) varied the above experimental design and, although failing to replicate the differential effects of model competence, reported a positive relationship between social class and adherence to modeled self-reward standards.

Bandura, Grusec, and Menlove (1967) investigated the effects on rate of self-reinforcement of nurturance, peer and adult models, social reinforcement for stringent self-imposed standards, and the subject's sex. The bowling task was again employed and tokens redeemable for prizes were used as rewards. Subjects observed an adult model who was either nurturant (warm, friendly) or nonnurturant (cold, detached) performing the task, verbalizing evaluations of his own performance, and occasionally awarding himself tokens. For some subjects, a supplementary peer model displayed standards conflicting with those set by the adult model—that is, he rewarded himself for minimal performances despite the fact that the adult model rewarded himself only after high performance scores. After the modeling phase, half of the subjects observed the adult model receive social praise from the experimenter for having adopted such stringent standards. The results of this experiment showed that children who had been exposed to the adult model and had witnessed his social reinforcement for high standard setting were much more likely to adopt stringent self-reward criteria than subjects who had observed a conflicting peer model. The nurturance of the model had a tendency to produce more lenient standards. There were no significant sex differences. The most stringent achievement criteria were adopted by children who had witnessed a nonnurturant adult model performing in the absence of a conflicting peer model and receiving praise for his austere standards.

Further evidence for the influence of social learning factors in the acquisition of self-reward patterns was reported by Mischel and Liebert (1966). They employed the bowling task and redeemable tokens in an investigation of the effects of discrepancies between self-imposed and externally imposed reinforcement standards. Children initially interacted with an adult model who (1) adopted stringent self-reward criteria but encouraged the subject to adopt lenient standards, (2) adopted lenient criteria but imposed stringent ones on the subject, or (3) both adopted and imposed stringent self-reward criteria. Half of the subjects then demonstrated the game to another child after which they performed it alone, while the other half performed alone prior to their demonstration to the second child. The results indicated that consistency between the model's self-imposed standards and those that were imposed on the subject led to significantly more stringent self-imposed criteria. The standards that subjects imposed on other children tended to be identical to those to which they themselves adhered.

The importance of consistency between modeled and prescribed standards was further demonstrated by Rosenhan, Frederick, and Burrowes (1968), who asked children to participate in a bowling game with an adult model. Four experimental conditions were employed: (1) consistent-strict, in which the model awarded himself redeemable tokens only for high scores and imposed similar criteria on the child, (2) consistent-lenient, in which the model imposed low criteria on himself and the child, (3) child-indulgent, in which the model self-imposed high standards but encouraged the subject to adopt low standards, and (4) self-indulgent, in which low criteria were adopted by the model but high standards were imposed on the child. When subjects were later encouraged to play the game by themselves, highly significant variations were observed in their self-imposed standards. Children in the two consistent modeling conditions tended to adopt those criteria that they had previously observed. Subjects in the child-indulgent condition consistently adhered to the lenient norms that they had been encouraged to adopt. However, children who had been instructed to adhere to high standards, despite the model's lenient self-reward, displayed the most extreme violation of both stringent and lenient criteria. Although these findings are at mild variance with those of Mischel and Liebert (1966), they do add support to the contention that social learning processes and discrepant standards can have considerable impact on the development and maintenance of self-control patterns.

The above inquiries represent some of the classic and pioneering research on the role of social learning influences in the development of self-reward patterns. Subsequent investigators have extensively replicated and expanded these findings. For example, Liebert and his co-workers (Liebert & Allen, 1967; Liebert & Ora, 1968; McMains et al., 1969; Allen & Liebert, 1969a, 1969b) have explored the effects of reward magnitude and type of training (e.g., live versus filmed models). These investigators (Hill & Liebert, 1968; McMains & Liebert, 1968; Liebert, Hanratty, & Hill, 1969) have also replicated the previously discussed effects of inconsistent (discrepant) modeling and have shown that concrete, explicit descriptions of self-reward standards lead to more consistent performance.

As mentioned earlier, most of the research in the social learning paradigm has addressed itself to various observational (modeling) factors in the acquisition of self-rewarding responses. One exception to this generalization is a classic study comparing the relative effects of external and self-reinforcement in the maintenance of effortful behavior. Bandura and Perloff (1967) asked elementary students to perform a manual wheel-turning task; tokens redeemable for prizes were used as rewards. Subjects were divided into four groups: (1) self-reward, (2) external reward, (3) incentive control, and (4) control. Self-reward subjects were instructed to choose their own performance standards and to award themselves tokens whenever they attained those standards. The wheel-turning apparatus was constructed such that a set number of wheel rotations illuminated different score indicator lights (eight rotations were required to illuminate the first, sixteen for the second, twenty-four for the third, and thirty-two for the fourth). Subjects chose their self-reward standard by moving a criterion-selector switch to the appropriate position. After their initial criterion choice, self-reward subjects were allowed to change their chosen standard only once. Children in the second group, the external reward group, were individually yoked to self-reward subjects, such that they received externally administered rewards equivalent in magnitude and performance standards to those self-administered by children in the first group. Thus external reward subjects experienced reinforcement conditions identical to those of self-reward subjects, except that their performance criteria and rewards were controlled by the experimenter rather than by themselves. In the third group, the incentive control condition, children were likewise yoked to a self-reward subject in that they received an identical amount of externally administered tokens. However, in this group, the tokens were awarded to them en masse at the beginning of the session, a procedure designed to control for the possible influence of receiving any form of reinforcement in the experiment. The fourth group, a second control group, did not receive any reward whatsoever but was asked to perform the wheel-turning task. The dependent measure was number of wheel-turning responses performed before terminating the activity. The results showed that subjects in both the external and self-reward conditions maintained their performances significantly longer than children in the two control groups. With the exception that boys performed more wheel-turning responses when they were externally rewarded, the two reinforcement systems were equally effective in maintaining effortful responding. A particularly interesting finding was that subjects in the self-reward condition frequently imposed very stringent performance standards on themselves. Indeed, one third of these children actually raised their initially high performance criteria such that they required even more work from themselves prior to each self-reward! In order to test the possibility that the self-selection of performance goals may have accounted for the behavior maintenance of self-reward subjects, a second study (Bandura & Perloff, 1967) was performed. Subjects either chose their own achievement goals or had them imposed by the experimenter. Neither of these groups received tokens. Their performances, which did not differ, were dramatically poorer than that of self-reward subjects. The above findings—that self-administered rewards have an effect equivalent to that of externally presented ones—were subsequently replicated by Liebert, Spiegler, and Hall (1970). As we shall see in the next section, clinical applications of self-reward have also suggested this equivalence.

The basic generalizations that seem warranted by existing research on the social learning of self-reward patterns include the following:

1. Self-rewarding behaviors may be established through exposure to models.
2. Self-imposed standards of reinforcement are affected by previous modeling experiences.
3. Discrepancies between the competencies of a model and a subject may attenuate the extent to which modeled standards are adopted.
4. Discrepancies between a model's self-imposed reward criteria and those that he imposes on a subject dramatically weaken the latter's subsequent adherence to even lenient self-reward standards. One possible exception to this generalization is that in which the discrepancy favors the subject.
5. Consistency between models enhances adoption of modeled self-reward standards.
6. The effects of socially learned self-reward patterns are basically equivalent to those of externally administered reinforcement systems in maintaining effortful responding.
7. When given the opportunity to choose or alter their own self-reward standard, subjects will often impose very high work requirements on themselves.

As with the directed learning paradigm, there is ample room for "analogue error" in generalizing the results of the social learning research conducted in laboratory settings to everyday applications. The failure to use clinically meaningful tasks is a common problem in both laboratory paradigms. Research on the social learning of self-reward patterns has been less frequently faulted for failing to employ discrete self-reward criteria and strong rewards. In addition, clinical relevance and validity of the Bandura *et al.* research has been upheld in several successful applications.

Before leaving our discussion of laboratory research on self-reward, mention should be made of several animal analogue studies in this area. Recall that the definition of positive self-reinforcement requires that an organism having free access to some reward indulges in that reward only after exhibiting some requisite performance. In contrast to conventional animal research in which some response produces reinforcement, the reinforcement in self-reward research is available regardless of the organism's performance.

Mahoney and Bandura (1972) reported a study in which they trained pigeons to peck a disc prior to feeding from a previously accessible source of grain. This pattern, which satisfies the procedural requirements for self-reinforcement, was produced by initially fading in a work requirement and mildly punishing undeserved self-feeding. During test phases, of course, no external constraints were placed on either the pigeons' pecking performances or their consumption of grain reinforcement. At the beginning of each test trial, grain was made freely available. If the pigeon pecked the disc prior to eating the grain, the sequence was scored as self-reward. When a disc peck did not precede eating, the sequence was labeled self-indulgence. Data from two pigeons revealed that a very consistent pattern of self-reinforcement can be established with brief training and, further, that these patterns are maintained for hundreds of trials after initial training has been terminated. Adherence to the optional work requirement of pecking prior to feeding was faultless for 1000 trials (20 days) in one subject. Even more interestingly, despite the fact that the pigeons did not have to peck at all prior to their feeding during the test phase, both pigeons not only continued pecking but actually increased the number of pecks they emitted prior to each self-reinforcement!

This latter finding suggested a second study (Mahoney & Bandura, 1972) in which a pigeon was asked to increase his work output prior to each self-reward. During initial training, the pigeon was mildly punished for attempting to feed if he had not attained a specified performance standard (one, two, three, four, or five pecks). Attainment of the standard was signified by the illumination of a white light. After the pigeon was consistently emitting five disc pecks prior to each feeding, the external punishment procedure was removed so that no response requirement existed. However, the white criterion light continued to operate. Gradually, the number of pecks needed to illuminate the criterion light was raised from five to six to seven and so on. Although the experimenters controlled the "standard" indicator, it should be remembered that the pigeon now had free access to the grain and was not required to emit any responses whatsoever. Nevertheless, the pigeon increased his performance to levels far exceeding those attained during training (cf. Figure 4–1). A rapid termination of the self-reward pattern then occurred and considerably less durable maintenance was exhibited after brief retraining.

Bandura and Mahoney (1973) and Mahoney, Bandura, Dirks, and Wright (1973), using this paradigm with a variety of responses and species, have replicated and extended the above findings. Congruent with our emphasis on the interdependence of external and self-control systems, these later studies have indicated that adherence to high self-reward standards is influenced by the frequency (scheduling) of external consequences for such adherence. The role of stimulus variables in controlling and enhancing maintenance of self-reward behaviors has also been investigated. Finally, the above laboratory analogue has been extended to monkeys and dogs in preliminary research on transfer of self-reward and preference for locus of control (external versus self-reinforcement). These animal studies, while undoubtedly suffering from several analogue errors in terms of clinical applications, highlight one of the points

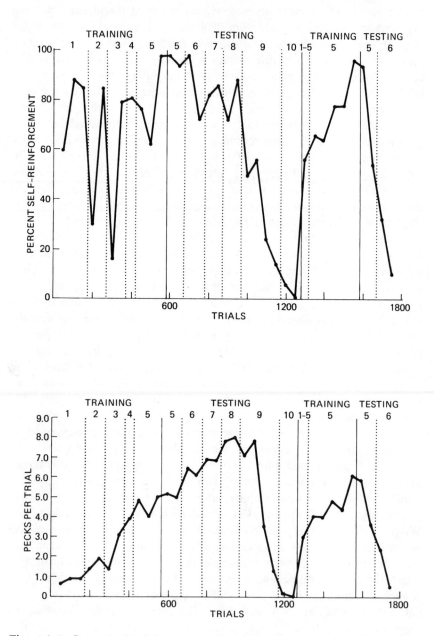

Figure 4–1   Rate of self-reinforcement and number of responses per self-reinforcement displayed by Pigeon 3. All data points in test trials represent responses in the presence of freely available grain and in the absence of punishment contingencies used in training. Numbers at the top of the graphs indicate the fixed-ratio schedules (performance standards) in effect during that period. (Adapted from Mahoney & Bandura, 1972.)

made in the first chapter—namely, that self-control phenomena involve complex behavioral sequences that are affected and maintained by environmental influences.

SELF-REWARD:
CLINICAL APPLICATIONS

In one form or another, self-reward operations have been a component in many clinical cases of self-regulation. More often than not, these applications have also involved other self-management strategies (e.g., stimulus control). The general philosophy of self-reinforcement has sometimes been presented to clients without too much attention to its actual implementation (e.g., Harris, 1969). In this section we shall discuss those applications in which self-reward procedures have received major emphasis.

As was the case with laboratory research, clinical applications of *negative* self-reward have been rare. Only one study has been reported to date in which subjects were instructed to remove contingently an aversive stimulus following the occurrence of some desired behavior. In a study that also employed stimulus-control strategies for the modification of obesity, Penick, Filion, Fox, and Stunkard (1971) devised the ingenious technique of having subjects store suet (pork fat) in their refrigerators and contingently remove pieces of it as they lost weight. The unsavory bags of fat, which were prominently displayed in the refrigerator, represented each subject's excess adipose. This negative self-reward was reported as being a very popular one and subjects who employed it in combination with stimulus-control techniques were very successful in their weight loss.

Studies in which positive self-reinforcement was a principal therapeutic technique are relatively numerous. Gutmann and Marston (1967) were among the first to report an attempted clinical application. In their study, subjects in an experimental group were told to treat themselves with cigarettes for having met a daily smoking reduction criterion. These smokers were told to reward themselves with one to three cigarettes if they had shown sufficient smoking control during the day. In addition to the self-awarding of cigarettes, experimental subjects employed self-recording, successive approximations of smoking control, and counterconditioning. Smokers in a control group self-recorded their daily cigarette consumption. This study suffered very high dropout rates and found no significant differences between the experimental and control groups.

Rehm and Marston (1968) treated male college students who had complained of anxiety in heterosexual relations. Experimental volunteers were assigned to one of three groups: (1) self-reinforcement, (2) nonspecific therapy, and (3) no-treatment control. Subjects in the latter two groups met for weekly interviews that were nondirective in nature. In the self-reinforcement condition, subjects were asked to construct graded hierarchies of hypothetical situations involving girls. Items on the hierarchy were arranged so that each item aroused slightly more anxiety than the preceding item. Subjects were subsequently told to record their progress in completing successive items on the hierarchy. They were also instructed to award themselves points and to engage in generous self-praise whenever they attained personal hierarchy goals. At their weekly meetings, subjects' records were discussed and verbal approval was given by the experimenter for high rates of positive self-evaluation.

Results of this investigation showed that self-reinforcement subjects displayed significantly better improvement than controls in their self-reports of both anxiety and actual overt behavior. Their performance in a standardized test situation was also superior to that of the other two groups. These improvements were maintained at a follow-up 7 to 9 months after the termination of the study. As Rehm and Marston point out, it is difficult to isolate which components of the self-reward therapy were most effective. However, their results suggest considerable promise for the clinical application of self-reinforcement strategies.

Comparisons between the effectiveness of external and self-reinforcement in the maintenance of naturalistic behaviors have been reported by several researchers. It will be recalled that this issue represents one of the more critical concerns in clinical applications of self-reward. Goodlet and Goodlet (1969) reported data from three disruptive ten-year-olds who, after baseline assessments, were externally rewarded for appropriate classroom behavior. Subsequent to this phase, each child was given the opportunity to reward his own performance. Data from a trained observer revealed that both reward systems were equally effective in controlling disruptive behavior. Additional evidence on the effects of teacher- and self-imposed reward contingencies were reported by Lovitt and Curtiss (1969). Following baseline measurements, an elementary student was awarded points for specified academic performances. These points were redeemable for special privileges. Specification of the reward contingencies was subsequently turned over to the student; that is, even though the teacher still dispensed the points, her rate of administering them was controlled by the subject. During a final phase, the teacher again assumed control over reinforcement contingencies. Results from this case study indicated that the student's performance was much better when he specified his own reward contingencies. A later experiment demonstrated that this superiority was not caused by greater leniency in self-imposed rather than teacher-imposed contingencies.

Further evidence for the functional equivalence of external and self-presented rewards is provided by Glynn (1970) in a study involving 128 ninth-grade girls. After a baseline assessment of students' performance in history and geography, a token reward phase was introduced. In one group, reward contingencies were experimenter-determined. A second group of students was allowed to specify their own contingencies, and a third "chance-determined" group was comprised of students whose rewards were made equivalent to those of a randomly selected self-reward subject. A no-reward control group was also included. These procedures varied from those used by Lovitt and Curtiss (1969) in that all tokens were self-administered; the groups differed only in the means by which the schedule of token presentation was established. For the external and chance groups, the token exchange values were not under students' control. This distinction between self-administration of reward and self-determination of reward contingencies is an important one to keep in mind (Morgan & Bass, 1971). Glynn found that self-determined reinforcement was equally as effective as external reinforcement in improving test performance. Consistent with previous laboratory findings, self-reward subjects tended to increase their self-imposed work requirements. A clinically noteworthy finding of this study was that subjects who initially received chance-determined rewards did very poorly when they were subsequently allowed to specify their own reinforcement standards. These data suggest that preliminary training procedures should emphasize consistent and concrete reward criteria.

One of the most impressive studies evaluating the effects of external and self-reward was reported by Bolstad and Johnson (1972). Selecting the four most disruptive children from each of ten first- and second-grade classrooms, four experimental procedures were evaluated: (1) external reward (ER group), (2) self-reward (SR_1 group), (3) self-reward plus maintained self-monitoring (SR_2 group), and (4) two no-treatment control (NR_1 and NR_2 groups). After a baseline assessment (Phase I) of the frequency of disruptive behavior, children in the three experimental groups were systematically rewarded with points for reducing their disruptiveness (Phase II); the points were exchangeable for prizes. Two of the experimental groups subsequently received self-reward training, while the third continued receiving external reinforcement (Phase III). During training, the students' self-presented points were checked on by the experimenters to insure accuracy. A test interval (Phase IV) was then conducted in which the external reward and control groups continued as before, but self-reward children were given full control over their own point dispensation. Finally, an extinction period (Phase V) was introduced in which all points were removed. One of the self-reward groups (SR_1), however, was asked to continue its self-monitoring of disruptive behavior during this interval. The results of this study (cf. Figure 4–2) indicated that both external and self-reward produced considerable reductions in disruptive behavior. Children who rewarded themselves were slightly more successful in this respect than were children who received only external reinforcement. These findings suggest that self-regulation procedures may offer a favorable alternative to conventional classroom control techniques in terms of effectiveness, practicality, and cost.

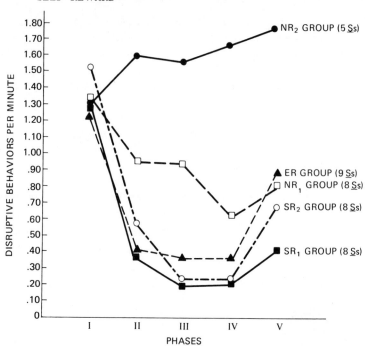

Figure 4–2   Average disruptive behavior per minute of groups. (Adapted from O. D. Bolstad & S. M. Johnson, "Self-Regulation in the Modification of Disruptive Classroom Behavior," *Journal of Applied Behavior Analysis*, 1972, 5(4), 447. Copyright 1972 by the Society for the Experimental Analysis of Behavior, Inc.)

A recent study by Jackson and Van Zoost (1972) has further demonstrated that self-reinforcement can be equally as effective as external reward in the improvement of college students' study habits. Moreover, follow-up data from their research suggested a long-term superiority on the part of self-reward subjects.

The foregoing studies have indicated that self-presented rewards and individual control over reinforcement contingencies can powerfully influence the academic and classroom behaviors of elementary as well as college students. In all of this research, self-reward was found to be at least as effective as external reinforcement in the development and maintenance of appropriate behaviors. There is, in fact, some preliminary evidence suggesting a slight superiority of self-reward with specified behaviors and subject populations. What with the crucial importance of durable improvement and generalization in behavior change projects, the auxiliary use of self-reward strategies to boost naturalistic maintenance may prove useful (e.g., Kaufman & O'Leary, 1972).

In addition to the above research on academic and classroom applications of self-reward, a variety of clinical studies have been reported. For example, Johnson (1971) and Mahoney (1971) used environmental planning plus self-reinforcement in the successful treatment of cases involving sexual fantasies, depression, and self-critical obsessions. Jackson (1972) also found that self-reward was effective in alleviating depression. An interesting clinical observation in the above case studies was that clients' self-evaluations and goals were very unrealistic. This point recalls Bandura's (1971b) speculation that depression and other forms of behavior pathology may be related to excessively stringent goal-setting and a preponderance of critical self-reactions.

Controlled group studies on the therapeutic effects of self-reward have also been reported. Beneke and Harris (1972), for example, combined self-reinforcement with a variety of other strategies in the successful improvement of college students' study habits. In the area of weight control, Mahoney and his colleagues (Mahoney, 1972b; Mahoney, Moura, & Wade, 1973) have found that self-reward significantly improved the effectiveness of self-monitoring and stimulus-control procedures. In one study (Mahoney, Moura, & Wade, 1973), the relative effects of self-reward, self-punishment, and self-monitoring were compared. All groups received information on stimulus-control procedures (see Chapter 1). To reinforce themselves, subjects in one group gave themselves money (self-reward) for the purchase of special items and entertainment. Self-punishment consisted of self-imposed fines (loss of money) for lack of weight-loss progress. Treatment data indicated that self-reward procedures were more effective than self-monitoring, self-punishment, or stimulus-control procedures alone.

In a subsequent study (Mahoney, in press), obese adults were equated for degree of obesity and randomly assigned to one of four groups. Subjects in three experimental conditions attended weekly weigh-ins and self-recorded their eating habits and body weight until the end of treatment. After a two-week baseline assessment, experimental subjects practiced different forms of self-control for a period of six weeks. Individuals assigned to a self-monitoring (SM) group set weekly goals for their weight loss and habit improvement. In addition to continued self-monitoring and goal-setting, subjects in two self-reward (SR) groups awarded themselves money or gift certificates whenever the one group (SR–Weight) attained weight loss or the other group (SR–Habit) habit improvement goals. Control subjects received no treatment, but, after the formal study was completed, they pursued a self-control program in which self-reward was made contingent on attainment of both habit and weight-loss goals. A follow-up assessment was conducted four months after the initiation of the program to assess the enduring effects of self-managed change. The results of this study are depicted in Figure 4–3. Self-reward was again found to be superior to simple self-monitoring. Moreover, self-presented reinforcements were more effective in producing weight reduction when they were made contingent on eating-habit improvements

"No! I absolutely refuse to buy any magazines."

"That was great! I finally said no to a salesman."

rather than weekly weight losses. Follow-up contacts after one year revealed wide individual variations in maintenance (ranging from slight gains by some subjects to a cumulative reduction of seventy-four pounds by one of the self-reward participants). These findings replicate those of previous research and highlight the significance of environmental support in long-term maintenance of self-change efforts.

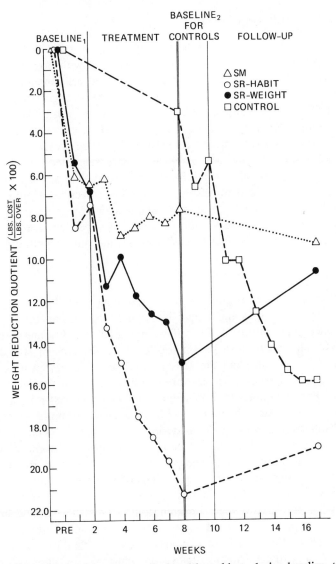

Figure 4–3 Median weight changes displayed by subjects during baseline, treatment, and follow-up phases. During Weeks 11–17, control subjects self-rewarded achievement of both weight loss and habit improvement goals. (Adapted from Mahoney, in press.)

The foregoing applications of self-reinforcement in clinical and educational settings demonstrate the therapeutic promise offered by these strategies. Although many issues and applications remain to be explored, the overwhelming conclusion to be drawn from the above research is that self-reward operations appear to be consistently useful in the treatment of a wide variety of behavior problems.

ISSUES IN SELF–REWARD

Not surprisingly, the relative density of research on self-reward has pointed up several focal issues. Many of them deal with possible generalizations from previous research employing external reinforcement. As we have seen in the last two sections, the evidence strongly suggests that reward systems are equally as effective when they are self-applied as when they are administered by some other agent. If it is true that the principles of self-applied reinforcement are congruent with those involved in external applications, several important implications are suggested. For example, the literature on schedules of reinforcement would then suggest that individuals should be trained to reward their performances on a progressively leaner schedule in order to maximize their behavior maintenance. Unfortunately, schedules of self-reinforcement have yet to receive much research interest. This is also the case with several other significant issues.

Nature of the Self-Presented Reward

Recall that self-reward is comprised of presenting oneself with a positive stimulus or removing some negative stimulus contingent on a desired performance. The nature of this self-manipulated stimulus merits consideration. In addition to such parametric issues as the type of stimulus, its intensity or magnitude, and the self-imposed schedule of reward, a very practical question arises as to the pretreatment status of the manipulated stimulus. For example, in applications of negative self-reinforcement, clients initially present themselves with an aversive stimulus in order to later self-remove it, contingent on desired performances (Penick, Filion, Fox, & Stunkard, 1971). This, of course, adds an early *aversive* component to self-regulatory efforts. The practical ramifications of this problem are further highlighted in some applications of positive self-reward: When the positive self-presented stimulus involves a new reinforcer (e.g., a long-awaited purchase, a special evening out), the self-regulation involves drawing upon *potential* reward sources. However, another reward source is comprised of those *current*, everyday situations that the person finds pleasant (e.g., coffee drinking, television viewing). In the case of the latter, a self-imposed state of deprivation must be employed (Premack, 1972). That is, the person must initially deny himself some pleasant everyday experience in order to use it as a contingent reinforcement for a desired behavior. This again requires a preliminary aversive component in the self-management enterprise. Whether this self-deprivation influences the initiation or maintenance of the self-reward pattern has yet to be explored. Likewise, no research has been reported on the relative promise of using potential self-rewards rather than current reinforcers. In preliminary case studies addressing the latter issue, Danaher (personal communication) has found some evidence for the superiority of the potential category.

It should be noted that the source of rewarding stimuli also requires some attention. In most applied instances, the individual is the source of his own reinforcements, either by depriving himself of current activities or by transforming potential reinforcers (e.g., money) into self-rewards. This differs from laboratory research paradigms in which the experimenter provides the individual with rewards. Whether the source of reward influences either the standards or the effects of self-imposed contingencies remains to be examined.

Applications of the Premack Principle

Another significant issue in self-reward concerns extrapolations from Premack's theory on reinforcement processes (Mahoney, 1972a). Briefly, the Premack Principle asserts that, given free access to various response options, those behaviors engaged in most frequently can be employed contingently as reinforcers for those engaged in less frequently (Premack, 1965, 1971). For example, if a child's spinach-eating is a low-probability behavior (LPB), but his television viewing is a high-probability behavior (HPB), the latter may be used to reward the former. This approach to motivation is very useful because it focuses on the *relativity* between two response probabilities. Before Premack's theorization, reinforcement theory was dominated by many stereotypes (e.g., that reinforcers were consummatory responses such as eating and drinking). By altering the moment-to-moment probabilities of two responses, Premack (1971) has shown that their reinforcement relationship can be reversed (e.g., when drinking is a HPB it will strengthen running responses, whereas when it becomes a LPB relative to running it will actually punish that performance).

In addition to this probability hypothesis, Premack has presented several auxiliary statements regarding the necessary and sufficient conditions for reinforcement. Among them have been a *contingency* and a partial reduction in the frequency of the HPB. According to Premack, HPBs serve as reinforcers for other, less probable responses only when their ad lib probabilities are reduced. If an HPB is made contingent on some response in such a manner that no HPBs are "lost" (i.e., there is no decrease from ad libitum level), no reinforcement effect is observed. This hypothesis has important implications for the previously discussed issue of self-deprivation. Specifically, Premack's hypothesis would predict that a state of partial self-deprivation is necessary for effective self-reinforcement. This extrapolation is perhaps less clear when potential rather than current HPBs are involved. However, the implication for clinical applications is that self-reward standards should not be so lenient as to produce no appreciable change in everyday reinforcers. As we have seen, the imposition of excessively stringent standards can likewise spell doom in applied instances. Judicious selection of realistic but modest performance standards appears to be the most reasonable recommendation. Further research is needed to clarify the validity and variables involved in extrapolating Premackian concepts to applied settings.

Another Premackian issue in self-management relates to the problem of determining response probabilities in naturalistic situations (Mahoney, 1972a). In Premack's theorization, the *probability* of a response must be distinguished from its *frequency*. To determine the former, a test situation must be developed in which no contingencies are placed on the response of interest. Many researchers employing the Premack Principle in self-management have mistakenly assumed that high-frequency responses possess the same reinforcement value as high-probability responses. However, a response that is frequently engaged in because of its contingent relationship to other motivational variables need not be reinforcing in and of itself. Taxpaying and domestic chores, although high-frequency behaviors, are not usually considered reinforcing. Nonetheless, mundane responses such as turning on a kitchen faucet and answering the telephone have been employed as contingent reinforcers (HPBs) in self-reward applications (Lawson & May, 1970). It is interesting to speculate whether the occasional success of these seeming misapplications may not have resulted from the high-frequency cueing function of the behaviors. For example, if a depressed housewife is told to engage in a positive self-thought prior to answering the telephone, the latter may well serve not to strengthen such thoughts but to serve as a *cue* for their occurrence. Danaher (in press) presents an excellent analysis of some of the problems encountered in Premackian extrapolations to self-control. The application of Premack's own conceptual and research skills in this area is doubtless a promising sign for the development of the field (Premack, 1970, 1972).

Two other issues that have been raised in this area deal with the generality of the probability–reinforcement relationship and the automatic nature of the reinforcement. Mahoney (1972a) has noted that some clinically relevant high-probability responses (e.g., obsessions, compulsions) present a paradox to Premack's theorization since they are reported by clients as being subjectively aversive. Whether these responses should be more properly labeled high-frequency behaviors due to their contingent relationship with motivational influences remains to be demonstrated.

An even more intriguing question concerns the frequently presumed automaticity of the reinforcement effect. Homme (1965) and others employing Premackian techniques in self-regulation have implicitly maintained that any response followed by a reinforcing event (HPB) will be automatically strengthened. Homme suggests that the individual obtain maximum benefit from daily reinforcers (coffee, cigarettes, etc.) by requiring accelerative behaviors to precede them. Skinner, however, has expressed doubts about the effectiveness of simply throwing desired behaviors in front or some preprogrammed reinforcer (Mahoney, 1970). Premack's own theorization would likewise discourage this if no decrement in the HPB took place. One of the interesting things about the automaticity issue relates to the effects of cognitive variables on reinforcement and stimulates several questions. Are the effects of a reward influenced by whether a person perceives it as being accidental or contingent? Does one's knowledge of the self-imposed nature of a contingency alter the effects of that contingency? These intriguing questions deserve the attention of researchers.

Other Issues in Self-Reward

In addition to the need for systematic explorations of the relative effects of various types of self-reward (positive versus negative, continuous versus intermittent), several other issues have been raised. Morgan and Bass (1971), for example, have called for more attention to the differences between self-administration of rewards and self-imposition of reward contingencies. This issue was raised by the research of Lovitt and Curtiss (1969) and Glynn (1970). In clinical applications, the two procedures are usually combined after initial instructions or therapist prompting. A related issue was addressed by Bass (1971), who hypothesized that self-reward operations do not possess behavior maintenance properties when expectations for external reinforcement are absent. In this research, evidence was found suggesting that subjects will adhere to stringent self-reward standards only when they anticipate social approval for doing so. This finding is, of course, consistent with the interdependence between self- and external-control systems that we have emphasized. Self-regulatory efforts will not be maintained in the continued absence of environmental support. However, the Bass (1971) findings do not seem to speak to the behavior maintenance functions of self-presented rewards.

These are just a few of the outstanding issues that await researchers in the area of self-reinforcement. However, as our review of clinical applications has shown, there can be little doubt that the technique of self-reward offers considerable therapeutic promise in the effective self-management of behavior.

Chapter

Self-Punishment
and Aversive
Self-Regulation

In marked contrast to the relatively large number of experimental studies on self-reward, comparatively little research has been conducted on self-punishment. As we shall see in our discussion, this relative imbalance might be reasonably attributed to the fact that self-control researchers have experienced differential consequences for their efforts in these two areas—that is, while some rather consistent success has been obtained in self-reward studies, only marginal and infrequent positive results have been demonstrated in the area of self-punishment. Before reviewing the major studies and findings in the latter, however, we shall turn our attention to the matter of definition and conceptualization.

THE CONCEPT OF
SELF–PUNISHMENT

As pointed out in Chapter 1, there are at least two major types of self-punitive strategies: (1) *negative self-punishment*, a condition whereby a person optionally self-administers some aversive stimulus following a targeted response, and (2) *positive self-punishment*, a condition whereby a person optionally removes a positive stimulus after a targeted response. In instances of human self-punishment, the target response is *decelerative* in the sense that the individual has verbalized the goal of reducing its occurrence.

Perhaps a better way of clarifying the concept of self-punishment is to contrast it with some other forms of aversive self-stimulation. For example, the self-destructive behaviors that are commonly reported in cases of autism (e.g., Lovaas, Freitag, Gold, & Kassorla, 1965) may be distinguished from self-punishment on several accounts. For one thing, there is no apparent decelerative response in self-destructive or masochistic behavior. Moreover, based on our earlier definition of self-control, the self-mutilating person is typically not engaging in a previously improbable response but, instead, is engaging in a self-stimulatory pattern usually with a history of relatively high frequency. Finally, the "motivational" contingencies governing masochistic and self-punitive response patterns are often markedly different. Lovaas and others have shown that the classical self-destructive patterns in autism are frequently associated with immediate environmental reinforcement. Schaefer (1970) has also reported that monkeys can be trained to bang their heads and produce lesions if this behavior is instrumentally reinforced. Sandler (1964) presents further evidence in an excellent review of experimental masochism, concluding that patterns of self-destructive behavior have usually been generated via some form of pairing with reinforcement. It would thus appear that self-punishment may be distinguished from other forms of aversive self-stimulation on the basis of at least four criteria: (1) the specification of a decelerative target response, (2) the presence of a self-imposed decelerative contingency, (3) the previous probability of the aversive self-stimulation, and (4) the immediate consequences of the pattern. Note that this does not mean that self-injurious behaviors may not be appropriately classified as some form of self-control. We shall discuss some of these other forms later in the chapter. Levine's (1973) remarks about the social relativity of how we label self-regulatory actions have particular relevance in this area.

A somewhat less marked but equally important distinction is that between self-punishment and the self-control patterns called *restraint* and *endurance.* A person displays restraint when he optionally delays, reduces, or foregoes some form of positive stimulation (e.g., the hungry dieter who turns down a piece of pie). By contrast, endurance is exhibited when a person optionally tolerates or intensifies some form of aversive stimulation (e.g., the fatigued athlete who ekes out one last push-up). Note that this definition of endurance is very similar to the phenomena we have been discussing as masochism and self-mutilation. Distinctions between the two, though somewhat arbitrary, are usually based on functionality, social desirability, and the conspicuousness of current motivating contingencies. A more useful differentiation is provided by the fact that restraint and endurance actually represent target behaviors (CRs) rather than self-controlling strategies (SCRs). As we shall see, restraint and endurance patterns are usually maintained by controlling responses (e.g., self-instructions, covert self-evaluation, etc.).

One final point that needs to be re-emphasized is that a behavior pattern is not classified here as self-punitive *unless* the person has immediate and direct control over the aversive stimulation. A preprogrammed punishment (e.g., Azrin & Powell, 1968) does not satisfy this requirement.

AVERSIVE SELF–REGULATION: ENDURANCE AND RESTRAINT

Recall that self-punishment represents a self-controlling response, whereas endurance and restraint are popular examples of self-controlled behaviors. Because of their important role in lay definitions, the latter two forms of self-control will be briefly discussed.

Endurance

Endurance may be defined as any instance in which an organism optionally tolerates or intensifies some form of aversive stimulation in the absence of any *immediate* external contingencies. The previous example of physical exercise well illustrates this form of self-control. When an individual engages in a strenuous exercise routine (in the absence of a drill instructor or other power-wielding agents), he is exhibiting a self-control pattern that often capitalizes on anticipated but delayed positive consequences. It is sometimes very difficult to distinguish endurance from some of the classical forms of behavior pathology illustrated in masochism and self-mutilation (cf. Sandler, 1964; Schaefer, 1970). In the latter actions an organism engages in aversive self-stimulation that may have a real or perceived pay-off in terms of social attention, alleged purification, and so on.

The fine line between socially condoned forms of aversive self-regulation (such as endurance) and pathological patterns of mutilation is well illustrated in a study by Sandler and Quagliano (1964). In a signal-avoidance paradigm, they initially trained monkeys to administer a mild shock to themselves in order to avoid a more intense experimenter-administered shock. At this point in the study, the monkeys' self-injurious behavior was very rational and functional in terms of current environmental contingencies. Sandler and Quagliano then gradually increased the level of the self-administered shock so that it was equal in intensity to that being avoided. Finally, they discontinued the second shock entirely so that no avoidance behavior was called for. Despite these changes in the prevailing environmental contingencies, the monkeys persisted in their painful self-stimulation. Not only did they continue self-shocking when the shock intensity was gradually increased, but they also continued their self-mutilation for hundreds of trials after the "avoided" shock had been removed. One monkey shocked himself almost 1900 times with the same intensity shock that he had previously worked to avoid. Congruent with the Sandler and Quagliano findings, Stone and Hokanson (1969) reported that human subjects not only continued to self-shock after this response had lost its functionality, but they also *increased* the aversive self-stimulatory pattern during an extinction phase.

The implications of such tenacity have been touched upon by Bandura (1971b) in terms of classical patterns of behavior pathology. A self-injurious or self-critical response system may be initially established and maintained through planned or adventitious environmental contingencies. However, the data suggest that such systems may be extremely tenacious (and dysfunctional) long after these initial conditions have been removed. The endurance of these aversive self-stimulatory patterns recalls Sandler's (1964) contention that such behavior patterns are frequently linked with intermittent reinforcement. Needless to say, in a culture in which self-criticism and self-abnegation are socially encouraged, self-control researchers might do well to explore ways by which these patterns might be avoided or altered. For example, one way is to help the person reduce the frequency of self-critical negative thoughts and increase positive self-thoughts (Mahoney, 1971; Hannum, Thoresen, & Hubbard, 1974). While self-critical patterns may be associated with superior performances in some realms (cf. Haynes & Kanfer, 1971), they certainly accompany and contribute to serious behavior disorders (Bandura, 1971b).

Still another illustration of endurance as a self-control pattern is provided by those studies dealing with "pain tolerance." These inquiries have dealt with the variables affecting an individual's ability to endure an aversive stimulus (e.g., Staub, Tursky, & Schwartz, 1971; Staub & Kellet, 1972). In these studies, endurance has been defined as the highest intensity endured prior to the individual's termination of the task (e.g., incremental electric shocks) or as the amount of time an individual will endure a relatively constant aversive stimulus (e.g., immersion of a hand in ice water). The degree of self-control exhibited in these studies is affected by the immediacy and magnitude of environmental consequences for performance. However, since the termination of the aversive event is placed in the hands of the individual, some self-regulation is involved.

In a series of experiments dealing with painful hand immersion in ice water, Kanfer and his colleagues (Kanfer & Goldfoot, 1966; Kanfer, Cox, Greiner, & Karoly, 1972; Kanfer & Seidner, 1972) have shown that an individual's ability to endure an aversive stimulus is enhanced by the provision of distracting stimuli, formal contracts, and anticipated reward. These findings re-emphasize our previous point that the self-regulatory phenomena labeled endurance and restraint are actually controlled responses (CRs) rather than self-controlling strategies (SCRs). Given an instance of either of these two patterns, one can usually identify concurrent maintaining strategies, that is, environmental planning or behavioral programming.

Restraint

Perhaps more than any other category, restraint is considered to be one of the cardinal forms of self-control. Indeed, as we mentioned in Chapter 1, restraint comprises for many a lay definition of self-control and plays a significant role in major conceptualizations in the area. Restraint is displayed when a person optionally delays, reduces, or foregoes some positive consequences. The investigation of resistance-to-temptation phenomena has long held the interest of self-management researchers (cf. Walters, Leat, & Mezei, 1963; Walters & Parke, 1964; Aronfreed, 1964, 1968; Walters, Parke, & Cane, 1965; Stein, 1967).

By far the most significant and extensive research on restraint has been carried out in the area of delay of gratification. This area is characterized by an experimental paradigm that asks the subject to choose between an *immediate small* reward and a *delayed but larger* reward. Note that this format epitomizes one of the self-control features discussed in Chapter 1, namely, the conflicting consequences of the two response options. If the individual chooses the immediate reward, a small but prompt gratification ensues at the sacrifice of a delayed but larger incentive.

The area of delay of gratification has been dominated by Mischel and his colleagues (e.g., Mischel & Metzner, 1962; Mischel & Gilligan, 1964; Bandura & Mischel, 1965; Mischel & Staub, 1965; Mischel & Masters, 1966; Mischel, Ebbesen, & Zeiss, 1972; Staub, 1972). The basic format in these studies has been one in which a child is asked to indicate his preference between two rewards (e.g., a pretzel and a marshmallow). After this, the child is asked to wait in an experimental room while the experimenter goes to another room to perform some alleged task. The child can bring the experimenter back at any moment by ringing a bell. He is told that if he beckons the experimenter with the bell, he immediately receives the less preferred reward. If he waits for the experimenter to return at his own pace, however, the more preferred reward is received. Length of the delay interval is employed as the dependent variable.

Considerable study has been done on the variables affecting delay of gratification. Mischel's research has dealt with the parameters affecting an individual's ability to delay gratification. To date, modeling and verbal persuasion have shown themselves to enhance delay ability. More interestingly, various attentional or distractive variables have been found to affect the duration of delay. What the child is thinking during the delay interval appears to be a very important factor (cf. Mischel, Ebbesen, & Zeiss, 1972). Thoughts about the delayed rewards or the actual presence of them seem to affect the ability to delay. The preliminary evidence suggests that restraint is enhanced in those situations where the individual does not think about the awaited rewards and where they are not physically present temptations. These findings are consistent with the findings of Kanfer and his colleagues (cited earlier) regarding distraction in pain tolerance. Moreover, they also blend well with the stimulus-control procedures found to be effective in weight control programs (see Chapter 1).

Stumphauzer (1970a, 1970b, 1972) has reported that the delay of gratification paradigm may be useful in designating and treating delinquents. In two studies he showed that delinquents' preferences for immediate or delayed rewards can be modified by social reinforcement and modeling. The clinical relevance of this extrapolation is certainly one deserving further exploration.

An interesting animal analogue to the delay of gratification paradigm was performed by Ainslee (reported in Rachlin, 1970) and further explored by Rachlin and Green (1972). They gave pigeons the choice between immediate but brief access to food reinforcement versus delayed but longer access. None of the pigeons acquired the delaying ability. However, congruent with the environmental programming we discussed in Chapter 1, it was found that the pigeons would work to avoid the choice point. That is, when given the opportunity to obtain their delayed (and larger) reinforcement by pecking a disc prior to the temptation (when both responses would have been available), pigeons consistently chose to prearrange the delayed reward and circumvent the subsequent choice. This intriguing illustration again points up the ability of animals to display self-regulatory patterns.

One final form of aversive self-regulation that deserves mention relates to the phenomenon of "countercontrol." There are many instances in which an individual may alter his behavior in a self-sacrificing direction as a means of controlling or influencing other's behaviors. As most parents and behavior-change specialists would agree, countercontrol is a seldom-cited but oft-observed phenomenon in everyday life. The child who declines conventional bedtime affection as a means of expressing discontent has been encountered by most parents at one time or another. Similarly, the emaciated prisoner-of-war who declines enemy-offered favors is exhibiting impressive self-regulation. Behavioral researchers are familiar with the occasional experimental subject who will go to great pains and personal sacrifice in order to perform contrary to the experimenter's wishes simply to demonstrate countercontrolling abilities (e.g., Mahoney, Thoresen, & Danaher, 1972). Although the immediate consequences in these situations are often hard to determine (e.g., would acquiescence in any of the above examples have placed the individual in a subjectively repugnant category?), the exhibition of some degree of self-control seems unquestionable. The relevance of countercontrol phenomena for self-regulation research remains to be explored (cf. Davison, 1973).

SELF–PUNISHMENT:
LABORATORY ANALOGUES

The relative deficit in self-punishment inquiries is particularly evident when laboratory studies are reviewed. Few studies have been reported wherein a person was brought into a laboratory situation and asked to present himself with a strongly aversive stimulus (e.g., shock) contingent on the occurrence of some designated behavior to be reduced. A much more popular analogue has dealt with the development and maintenance of self-criticism.

The area of negative self-evaluation has, of course, been one of long-standing interest to psychologists and its development has received some attention in the social psychological literature (e.g., Stotland & Zander, 1958). Researchers in the fields of learning and personality have also been quite interested in the functional value of self-criticism. Hill (1960), for example, discussed the role of negative self-evaluation in avoiding subsequent external castigation. Confessions of wrongdoing often illustrate this point. Aronfreed (1964, 1968) has also postulated that self-criticism serves an anxiety-reduction function because it employs words that have been previously associated with the termination of external punishment.

Much of the research dealing with laboratory analogues to self-punishment has resulted from the vicarious learning paradigm of Albert Bandura. In 1964, Bandura and Kupers reported data from a study investigating the effects of modeling on the transmission of self-reward patterns. Among other findings, they observed that experimental subjects expressed more subsequent evaluations of their own performance than did control subjects ($p < .01$). Indeed, 27 percent of the experimental subjects exactly reproduced the self-approving and self-critical verbalizations of the models. The implication is, of course, that self-evaluations are learned responses that can be transmitted via social and observational processes.

Grusec (1966) investigated some of the antecedents of verbal self-criticism with eighty kindergarten students. Subjects played a game and were subsequently punished for their performance. Termination of punishment was made contingent or noncontingent on the occurrence of verbal self-criticism on the part of the child. Contingent (negative) reinforcement facilitated the development of self-criticism. These results support the notion that self-critical responses are functionally related to their consequences.

Pursuing the implications of the earlier Bandura and Kupers (1964) findings, Thelen (1969) investigated the effects of modeled reactions to failure. Subjects observed a modeling film wherein an adult reacted to failure by emitting verbal self-criticism or by offering excuses ("rationalization"). Control subjects did not observe a model. In a subsequent card-sorting task of great difficulty, subjects were observed for their self-reactions. Those who had observed a self-critical model were significantly more critical of themselves than control subjects.

Kanfer, Marston, and their colleagues have also explored the development and effects of self-punitive responses using a directed learning paradigm (see Chapter 4). In most of these studies subjects' self-critical responses consisted of illuminating a light signifying an incorrect response. One of the earliest of these inquiries investigated the relationship between self-criticism and psychometric measures of intropunitiveness (Marston & Cohen, 1966). A visual discrimination task was employed. The results showed that individuals who scored in the middle range of intropunitiveness were more self-critical than those who scored high or low. Moreover, the data revealed that subjects' symbolic self-criticisms had a suppressive effect on the responses that they followed. Subsequent research in the directed learning paradigm has examined the relationship between symbolic self-reward and self-punishment (e.g., Kanfer & Duerfeldt, 1967a, 1968b; Kanfer, Duerfeldt, & LePage, 1969). Data from these later inquiries have suggested that (1) verbal self-evaluations may be independent of actual self-punitive responses, (2) self-reward and self-punishment may represent two independent response systems (i.e., a low self-rewarder is not necessarily high in self-punishment), and (3) although self-reward rates tend to match previous training schedules of reinforcement, self-punishment rates tend to be less than previous external punishment schedules. All three of these generalizations, of course, may have important clinical implications. Changing a client's verbal behavior does not necessarily mean that his self-punitiveness has been decreased. Likewise, increasing his rate of self-reward may have no effect on his self-criticism (Hannum, Thoresen, & Hubbard, 1974).

A well-designed analogue to clinical self-punishment was reported by Herbert, Gelfand, and Hartmann (1969). In their study forty fourth-grade students were asked to participate in a project allegedly dealing with the development of a new children's game. The game, a miniature bowling apparatus, allowed the experimenters to control success experiences across subjects. Every child received twenty tokens at the beginning of play. The subjects were told that after each toss of the bowling ball they could redeem a token for an immediate prize (candies, pencils, or money), or they could relinquish the token by placing it in a container marked "Bad." Prior to playing the game, half of the subjects observed an adult model who fined himself for low scores. The results showed that children exposed to a self-punitive model fined themselves significantly more frequently than children who had not observed the modeling. Consistent with the hypothesis that they were adopting the performance standards that had been modeled for them, their self-punitive responses were more frequent after extreme rather than moderately low scores.

The foregoing studies illustrate the existing laboratory-based inquiries into self-punishment. With few exceptions, all have employed verbal and symbolic forms of aversive stimuli. The data from these investigations suggest that (1) self-punitive behavior patterns may be acquired observationally, (2) that they are affected by their consequences, and (3) that they may be at least partially independent of other measures of self-regulation. Kanfer and his co-workers have reported consistent declines in the rate of self-punishment when compared with previous external punishment. Although this decrement could be accounted for on the basis of corresponding declines in a targeted response, this has yet to be demonstrated. Indeed, as we turn our attention to clinical applications of self-punishment, the long-term suppressive effects of this self-control strategy will be seriously challenged.

SELF–PUNISHMENT: APPLICATIONS

Just as the area of self-reward is dominated by research and applications in *positive* self-reward, so is the area of self-punishment dominated by research and applications of the *negative* variety.

One of the earliest documented reports of a negative self-punishment application appeared in 1964 when McGuire and Vallance presented data from thirty-nine clients who had undergone a variant of aversion therapy. The clients reported undesirable behaviors, which included smoking, alcoholism, and sexual deviation. Their therapy consisted of training sessions wherein painful electric shock followed presentations of specific to-be-avoided stimuli. Many of the stimulus presentations were done imaginally; that is, the client was instructed to imagine himself in the problematical situation. For the majority of the clients, this procedure was self-administered. After having been instructed in the necessary operations, individual clients controlled both the presentation of the target stimulus and the application of electric shock. *In vivo* self-applications between therapy sessions were also employed. McGuire and Vallance summarized their treatment results by classifying patient outcomes on a five-point scale (discontinued treatment, no improvement, mild improvement, good improvement, symptom removed). Of the thirty-nine clients, twenty-two (56 percent) were placed in the two highest outcome categories. Smokers and sexual deviants reported substantially more improvement than alcoholics. Although their very brief article does not provide details on actual self-report data, maintenance of self-punishment applications, and so on, it was very influential in laying the groundwork for subsequent clinical applications of self-punishment.

Utilizing the portable shock apparatus devised by McGuire and Vallance, Wolpe (1965) treated a client who complained of severe drug craving. The self-applied shock was only temporarily successful in suppressing drug approach behaviors. A more successful case study was reported by Mees (1966a), who trained a client to suppress deviant sexual fantasies through self-administered shock.

Goldiamond (1965b) reported the use of a form of negative self-punishment in the treatment of stuttering. Nonfluent subjects pressed a button that produced aversive delayed auditory feedback (DAF). They were instructed to press the button only when they felt that they had stuttered while performing a reading task. This procedure showed consistent success in suppressing disfluencies.

The results of several group studies involving negative self-punishment have suggested that demand characteristics and placebo variables may account for a substantial amount of the observed behavior change. For example, Mees (1966b) compared the suppressive effects of three conditions: self-presented shock, two variations of breath-holding, and a placebo procedure in which subjects self-presented "subliminal electrical impulses" that could not be felt. Breath-holding was intended to provide a mild self-punishment. After subjects used these procedures for three weeks to reduce their smoking, the results showed that one of the breath-holding procedures was most effective while the other was least. Moreover, the placebo procedure was slightly *more* successful than actual self-shock! These findings have been replicated by several other researchers (e.g., Rutner, 1967; Keutzer, 1968; Ober, 1968; Lichtenstein & Keutzer, 1969; Tyler & Straughan, 1970), who have reported no differences between breath-holding or self-presented shock procedures and no-treatment, self-monitoring, or placebo-control groups.

One of the most convincing demonstrations of placebo effects in self-punishment was reported by Weingartner (1971). Forty-five hallucinating mental patients were divided into three groups: (1) self-administered shock, (2) placebo-shock, and (3) no-treatment control. Individuals in the first two groups were provided with small shock devices that automatically and unobtrusively counted the frequency of self-administrations. Subjects were instructed to shock themselves whenever they hallucinated. For placebo-shock subjects, no actual shock was given, but patients were told not to worry if they did not feel anything since the current was designed "to activate the nervous system." After two weeks of treatment, all three groups showed improvement and there were no significant intergroup differences. It was concluded that the main agent of change was patient expectation rather than actual treatment technique. These data suggest that nonspecific variables may be at work in many applications of self-punishment.

A handful of case studies has been reported in which negative self-punishment procedures were found helpful. For example, Bucher and Fabricatore (1970) described the successful use of self-administered shock, again, in the suppression of hallucinations by a psychiatric patient. Some degree of relapse was reported within two months after treatment. Mahoney (1971) asked an out-patient diagnosed schizophrenic to punish self-critical obsessions by snapping a heavy-guage rubberband against the inside of his wrist. Reported obsessions declined to zero, and, after a subsequent treatment strategy (response priming and self-reward), no relapses were reported after four months had elapsed. In three cases where desensitization had failed to effect improvement, Rubin, Merbaum, and Fried (1971) used self-presented shock. Substantial success was reported in two of the cases and partial success in the third. Using a multiple baseline design, Morganstern (in press) asked an obese nonsmoker to punish candy, cookie, and doughnut eating by inhaling aversive cigarette smoke (see Figure 5–1). This procedure resulted in a weight loss of 53 pounds over twenty-four weeks.

It is, of course, impossible to isolate the active treatment components in any of the above case studies. However, as many clinicians will attest, the empirical question of which variable had an effect does not have as much practical significance as the fact that a therapeutic effect was observed.

The foregoing studies constitute the existing research on negative self-punishment. Their findings seem to indicate wide variability in success with the bulk of the evidence disfavoring negative self-punishment as an effective and enduring strategy for behavior change. It should be noted, however, that many of the more pessimistic studies have shared one important characteristic, namely, that they have dealt with the modification of smoking behavior. As Bernstein (1969) has pointed out, this target behavior appears to be one of the most difficult to alter. However, even excluding the smoking research, the therapeutic effects of negative self-

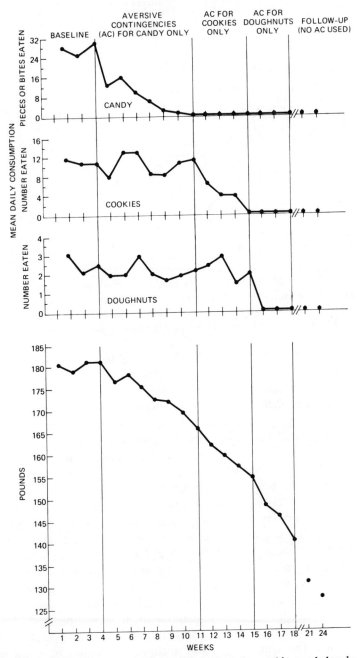

Figure 5-1 *Above*, mean daily consumption of candy, cookies, and doughnuts as a function of aversive contingency application. *Below*, weight as a function of aversive contingency applications to candy, cookies, and doughnuts. (Adapted from Morganstern, in press.)

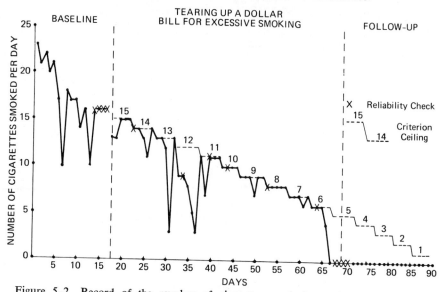

Figure 5–2   Record of the number of cigarettes smoked per day by Subject I. (From *Self-Control: Power to the Person*, by Michael J. Mahoney and Carl E. Thoresen. Copyright © 1974 by Wadsworth Publishing Company, Inc. Reprinted by permission of Brooks/Cole Publishing Company, Monterey, California, and the authors.)

punishment remain very obscure. Studies have either reported little or no success or have involved individual case histories that were not controlled for other possible variables. In short, there is little evidence to support the generalization that negative self-punishment is an effective clinical technique. Until more supportive research data are reported, this self-control strategy must be viewed with tentative pessimism.

The existing evidence on *positive* self-punishment is very brief. Axelrod, Hall, Weis, and Rohrer (1974) reported two case histories in which the subjects were told to punish themselves via reinforcement withdrawal as a means of reducing their smoking frequency. The subjects were two of·the authors (Weis and Rohrer). In the first case, the subject recorded a baseline smoking frequency and then imposed a daily limit of 15 cigarettes. For each cigarette that exceeded the limit, the subject was instructed to tear up a dollar bill. The limit was decreased by one cigarette every five days. After fifty days, the subject's smoking rate had decreased to zero and remained there at a two-year follow-up. Interestingly, the subject never exceeded his daily limit during the treatment phase. Although the self-punishment contingency existed, a self-punitive operation was never required. This case study is also worth noting because of its use of a changing criterion design (see Chapter 2). The authors report a correlation of 0.73 ($p < .001$) between the daily limit and the number of cigarettes smoked. This strongly suggests that it was, in fact, the limit setting and/or self-imposed contingency that caused the reduction in smoking.

In the second case study, the subject recorded baseline data and was then instructed to fine herself for each cigarette smoked by contributing 25 cents to charity. This technique was later supplemented by environmental planning instructions to avoid even purchasing cigarettes. A second brief baseline phase showed some reversal. One year follow-up data indicated occasional smoking. However, since the second subject began the study with a smoking rate of only 8.4 cigarettes per day, her follow-up data must be interpreted as indicating at least partial relapse.

The second investigation bearing on positive self-punishment is that reported by Mahoney, Moura, and Wade (1973), which compared the relative effectiveness of self-reward, self-punishment, and self-monitoring in the treatment of obesity (see Chapter 4). Five groups were involved: (1) self-reward, (2) self-punishment, (3) self-reward plus self-punishment, (4) self-monitoring, and (5) information control. All subjects received information on stimulus-control techniques for obesity (Stuart, 1967). In this study, self-punishment consisted of voluntarily relinquishing money for having failed to make weight reduction progress. After four weeks of treatment, subjects in the self-punishment group failed to show any more improvement than no-treatment control subjects. Four-month follow-up data indicated that subjects who used only positive self-punishment had shown significantly less improvement than subjects who had combined this technique with positive self-reward. The largest weight reductions were reported by individuals who combined systematic self-punishment and self-reinforcement. These findings again suggest a complementarity between the principles governing external and self-administered incentives. Consistent with Bandura's (1969) review of the punishment literature, it appears that self-administered punishment may be most effective when (1) positive rather than negative punishment is used, and (2) this strategy is combined with a systematic self-reward procedure. This emphasis on the simultaneous development of appropriate behaviors that are incompatible with the undesired performance has been very scarce in self-punishment applications. Further research will, of course, be required to evaluate the above tentative generalizations.

With only two existent investigations of positive self-punishment,[1] it

---

[1] Hauck and Martin (1970) report a study that they describe as involving "patient-controlled duration of time-out" from positive reinforcement. Time-out, of course, is a variety of positive punishment in which the opportunity to earn reinforcement is temporarily removed following the occurrence of an undesired behavior (Bandura, 1969; Kazdin, 1972). Since the optional self-removal of a reinforcing situation is herein considered a form of positive self-punishment, the Hauck and Martin study would appear to be very relevant. However, upon looking at their methodology, it will be seen that the study did not involve self-punishment as we have defined it. They treated a 59-year-old female schizophrenic who exhibited several objectionable mannerisms. The treatment consisted of having the patient listen to her favorite music (Ernie Ford hymns). Whenever she exhibited any of the targeted mannerisms during the listening sessions, *the experimenters terminated the music* and did

is impossible to draw any conclusions regarding the promise of this strategy in clinical applications. However, if one can extrapolate from general behavior principles, it would seem very likely that self-applications of positive punishment will be more effective than negative punishment. This is based on the wealth of evidence indicating that the removal of a reinforcer may be a more effective and less problematical form of punishment than the presentation of an aversive stimulus (Bandura, 1969). The findings of Mahoney, Moura, and Wade (1973) likewise suggest that positive self-punishment may be most effective when it is systematically combined with a positive self-reward system.

The effectiveness of any self-control program is affected not only by the power of the specific techniques it uses, but also by the consistency with which the individual implements them. Thus the rather sporadic outcome data reported in self-punishment studies may reflect inconsistencies

---

not present it again until the patient ceased exhibiting the mannerism. In one sense, the patient could indeed control the duration of time-out simply by controlling the duration of her transgressive behavior. However, since she did not have direct control over the administration and removal of the reinforcer (she could not, for example, occasionally override the experimenter-determined contingencies), self-punishment was not involved. The authors' labeling error is akin to that discussed in Chapter 1, wherein an individual attributed self-control to the rat since he could "choose" to respond or not to respond in the Skinner box.

in application rather than impotence on the part of the operations. If a subject or client does not "follow-through" consistently in the application of a strategy, one would not expect improvement. This issue has been termed the "contract problem" (Mahoney, 1970), and it poses a major challenge to self-control workers. Kanfer and Karoly (1972a) have presented an excellent analysis of some of the variables that may affect actual follow-through in a self-control enterprise.

Although the contract problem is relevant to all forms of self-regulation, it is particularly germane in the area of self-punishment and aversive self-regulation. The reason for this is that these self-control forms involve immediate and avoidable aversive stimulation. Theoretically, the ultimate positive consequences of reducing some undesired behavior are assumed to maintain self-punitive patterns. If the self-applied aversive stimulation is very intense, however, the individual may avoid its self-administration and thereby abandon his behavior change attempt. If, on the other hand, the stimulation is guardedly mild in order to insure self-application, it may lose its suppressive effects.

One of the most important implications of the contract problem is that self-control researchers should devote more empirical attention to the consistency with which self-management operations are applied. Without such consistency data, it is difficult to interpret the significance of reported changes in a target behavior. A few researchers (e.g., Axelrod, Hall, Weis, & Rohrer, 1974; Mahoney, in press; Mahoney, Moura, & Wade, 1973) have reported consistency findings. There is, therefore, a pressing need for the collection of data on the actual self-administration of techniques (see Chapter 2).

The last three chapters have reviewed discrete, overt strategies for controlling one's actions. However, as we have noted, many covert (cognitive) processes enter into virtually all instances of human self-regulation. An individual does not alter the consequences of his behavior without engaging in covert self-instructions, self-evaluation, and a variety of symbolic self-reactions. Anticipated consequences and cognitive labels play a critical role in human behavior. Despite our differentiation of individual self-regulatory strategies, the reader should bear in mind that complex combinations of a variety of processes are involved in naturalistic self-control. The next chapter will explore the promise and rich diversity of covert processes in human self-regulation.

Chapter

6

Covert
Self-Control

The influence of thoughts and images on human action has been repeatedly documented in history and literature. Prayer represents one example of a covert procedure aimed not only at communicating with the supernatural but also providing relaxation and self-instruction. Shakespeare often used covert or internal conversations to convey how a character was struggling to bring his behavior under control. Strategies for changing covert behaviors have likewise been extensively documented. *The Bhagavad Gita*, for instance, written over 2000 years ago, contains a wide variety of methods for controlling thoughts, images, and physiological processes.

Popularized strategies for self-change have placed heavy emphasis on the identification and improvement of significant covert events. Émile

Coué, for example, in the 1920s popularized a technique called *autosuggestion* in which individuals were taught to subvocalize positive statements such as the famous "Everyday in every way I am getting better and better." Dale Carnegie (1948), Norman Vincent Peale (1960), and Maxwell Maltz (1960) have also advocated the "power of positive thinking," along with a variety of techniques utilizing covert self-praise, modeling, and self-instructions.

The scientific status and clinical promise of these cognitive behavior change methods have only recently been examined. This rather belated investigation of covert processes by behavioral researchers is due to two factors: (1) There has been an implicit assumption that private events (thoughts, feelings, etc.) are somehow immune to the predictability and control that characterize overt responses, and (2) until recently, many researchers felt that cognitive processes were somehow "soft," unscientific, and necessarily vague. Fears were expressed about reopening the mind–body controversy, volitional and homunculus theories of human action, and so on. The methodological behaviorist recalled the hard-fought battles with introspective "mentalists" and generalized the assault to anything even suggestive of cognitive events. It is interesting to note that part of the reluctance of early behavioral researchers to address themselves to cognitive processes was attributed to B. F. Skinner's influential views. It has been a generally accepted notion that Skinner does not admit any need for private events in the experimental analysis of behavior. However, his views on the matter have been very explicit:

> When we say behavior is a function of the environment, the term "environment" presumably means any event in the universe capable of affecting the organism. But part of the universe is enclosed within the organism's own skin. . . . A small part of the universe is private (1953, p. 257).

Although Skinner has consistently acknowledged that covert processes can influence human behavior, he has frequently warned researchers to employ extreme rigor and caution in their investigations of covert responses. Since private phenomena must be inferred from other data sources (e.g., verbal reports), the researcher is at least one step removed from his dependent variable. Skinner has also cautioned investigators about the possible pitfalls of using circular "mentalistic" concepts in analyses of behavior, and many researchers have unfortunately misunderstood Skinner's remarks. His cautionary message has been interpreted by some as a proscription to totally avoid covert response processes. Not only does such avoidance limit one's knowledge and predictive power, but it also misrepresents Skinner's actual view on the role of private events in experimental research: "An adequate science of behavior must consider events taking place within the skin of the organism . . . as part of behavior itself

(1963, p. 953)." Clearly the experimental analysis of behavior need not stop at the boundary of the skin.

Recent developments in behavioral research have emphasized the long overdue need for controlled inquiries into cognitive-symbolic processes. Differentiating between radical (metaphysical) and methodological behaviorism, investigators have come to realize that these cognitive processes can be studied, predicted, and controlled with the same precision as external events. Homme (1965), in a classic position paper, categorized thoughts as "covert operants" (or "coverants") and invited behaviorists to tackle this forbidden area. He pointed out that the exclusion of cognitive processes from the experimental analysis of behavior not only limits its scope but also reinforces the very dualism that many (but not all) behaviorists criticize. Private behaviors are qualitatively no different from nonprivate ones. If man is a biological organism and thoughts, images, and feelings are neurochemical responses, then these latter events may be brought within the realm of behavioral science. To say that they are unresearchable is both premature and unjustified. A thought is not totally "unobservable"—its nature and occurrence are perceived by a public of one. By training the individual to be a personal scientist, covert events can be studied and controlled in much the same manner as overt behaviors (Thoresen, 1973a). Extending this argument, Mahoney (1970) pointed out that many of the behaviorist's fears about delving into cognitive processes are unjustified. By anchoring one's inference in observable criteria, adhering to direct inferences, and establishing operationally testable methods for evaluating covert phenomena, cognitive variables can become justifiable elements in behavior analysis. Moreover, the early exclusion of mental phenomena was argued on the basis of their lack of utility in predicting, controlling, and explaining behavior. A good practical criterion for evaluation of covert behaviors, then, is whether they prove useful in understanding behavior.

Bandura (1969) and others (Bower, 1970; Kanfer & Phillips, 1970; Staats, 1972) have offered very convincing evidence that covert processes are not only useful but *essential* in the understanding of complex human behavior. As the studies reviewed in this chapter will indicate, bringing private events into the realm of applied science offers an excitingly comprehensive perspective. Theories that emphasize either covert (cognitive) or overt (environmental) determinants of behavior to the exclusion of all others have not been very successful in accounting for the breadth and variability of human action. A comprehensive theory must incorporate both of these significant influences.

The basic premise of what might be called "covert behavior modification" (Mahoney, Thoresen, & Danaher, 1972) is that internal phenomena such as thoughts, images, and physiological actions can be viewed as responses similar to external behavior. Further, these phenomena are seen as susceptible to the same empirically derived laws and principles as overt or public events. This presumed correspondence between the principles governing overt and covert action is termed the continuity or homogeneity assumption. Its validity and usefulness are supported by several lines of evidence (e.g., Miller, 1959; Barber & Hahn, 1964; Bridger & Mandel, 1964; Bandura, 1969).

In terms of their effects on human action, covert behaviors may serve several functions. They may act as *antecedents* that cue the occurrence of other responses (e.g., smoking urges). Private events may also represent target *behaviors* in themselves due to their significant role in adjustment (e.g., hallucinations). Finally, covert behaviors may function as *consequences* of other actions (e.g., self-critical thoughts). Since overt events can also serve these three functions, several complex interactions are possible. Figure 6–1 presents the possible combinations of overt and covert antecedents, responses, and consequences. The complexities of categorization are enhanced by the fact that a response may perform several functions at once. For example, a self-critical behavior may serve as a consequence to one's weight gain, a response component of one's depression, and as a cue for subsequent dieting. Despite the seemingly clear-cut distinctions portrayed in Figure 6–1, it is often impossible to differentiate covert stimuli, covert responses, and covert consequences. Their functional

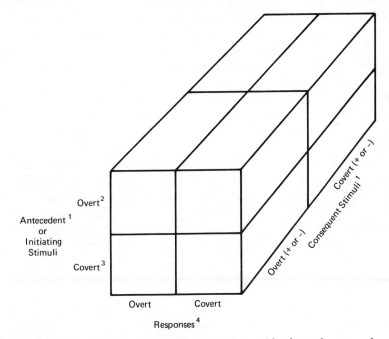

Figure 6–1 Classification system showing possible combinations of overt and covert antecedents, responses, and consequences.

interdependence both among themselves and within a myriad of external events requires a moment-to-moment classification system that identifies their immediate role in behavior change.

In an effort to impose some facilitative organization on this complex topic (Bower, 1970), our discussion of covert self-control will follow the format of the above classification system. Internal responses will be discussed in terms of their role as (1) antecedents, (2) target behaviors, and (3) consequences. The reader should keep in mind that this rather simplified and often arbitrary organization is solely for the purpose of effective communication—in naturalistic instances of covert self-control, such functional distinctions are rarely simple.

COVERT BEHAVIORS
AS ANTECEDENTS

In this section we shall deal with studies involving covert cues for subsequent behavior. A large body of research evidence has supported the notion that thoughts, images, and physiological events can gain stimulus control over a wide range of complex behavior. Indeed, as Bandura (1969) points out, there is reason to believe that a substantial amount of human learning is mediated by cognitive-symbolic processes. The flight-phobic individual, for example, may avoid airplanes not because of some reflexive association between airplanes and autonomic arousal but because of symbolic mediating responses that serve to self-arouse (e.g., imagery of a plane crash, recalling a recent newspaper article on air traffic problems, etc.). As we shall see in the next section, many problematical behaviors can be altered by systematically modifying the covert response patterns that precede them. In these strategies, the critical cueing value of covert events has resulted in their becoming the direct target of behavior change.

Our present discussion will deal with attempts to modify responses to covert events. Many of these methods have capitalized on the response approximation aspect of covert behaviors. As outlined in the previous section, thoughts and images are considered to be qualitatively similar responses to overt actions. They may represent early elements in a lengthy response chain that gradually becomes overt. Other covert events may function as structural plans (Miller, Galanter, & Pribram, 1960) that store information on critical performance elements (e.g., street directions). By working with the very portable and manipulable cognitive elements of a problem behavior (e.g., images of a feared situation), a therapist can produce very dramatic change.

The clinical relevance of covert antecedents and cognitive response approximations is well documented in the area of systematic desensitization (Wolpe, 1958). This technique represents one of the most frequently employed therapeutic strategies in behavior modification. In desensitization, clients are initially taught deep muscular relaxation. They are then asked to construct a graduated series (hierarchy) of feared situations. Low items on the hierarchy arouse very little anxiety from the client and only remotely resemble the actual feared situation (e.g., reading about an airplane crash). Subsequent items become progressively more fear-arousing until the terminal behavior is itself described (e.g., commercial flying). The client is trained to relax while imagining scenes from the hierarchy, and gradual progress is made from initial exposure to low anxiety items to actually imagining oneself in the targeted situation. In conventional desensitization, great care is taken not to arouse any anxiety during the "counterconditioning" process. Hierarchy items are arranged in very small transitions; any instances of arousal result in a procedural retreat back to a less anxious item.

Several investigators (e.g., Migler & Wolpe, 1967; Kahn & Baker, 1968; Marquis & Morgan, 1968; Donner, 1970; Suinn, 1970) have examined self-administered desensitization, in which a client is provided with taped or written instructions of muscular relaxation, hierarchy construction, and actual pairing procedures. The results of these studies have indicated that desensitizing procedures may be generally as effective when self-applied as when administered by a therapist. One possible problem in self-desensitization is that the individual may terminate the procedure prior to the attainment of his performance goal. Phillips, Johnson, and Geyer (1972), for example, reported a high attrition rate among clients using self-administered desensitization. This problem might be reduced by the use of formalized self-change contracts and by offering social approval or other positive consequences for maintenance.

Technical and conceptual variations on the desensitization procedure have recently been examined (e.g., Zeisset, 1968; D'Zurilla, 1969; Goldfried, 1971; Jacks, 1972; Menefee & Thoresen, 1973). For example, individuals have been trained to relax themselves not in response to imaginary feared situations but in response to physiological stress cues. The ability to self-induce relaxation then becomes a multipurpose self-control skill which need not be limited by a single performance theme. Suinn and Richardson (1971), for example, have developed a two and one-half hour training package for "anxiety management," which incorporates this general coping strategy of self-relaxation in response to internal stress cues. Meichenbaum and Cameron (1974) use a "stress inoculation" procedure that employs arousal cues as stimuli for relaxation and adaptive self-instruction. Preliminary research on this broad self-regulatory approach has suggested that it may offer substantial promise in terms of generalization, maintenance, and innovative self-applications.

Another therapeutic technique for the reduction of avoidance behaviors is that of "flooding," or "implosion." Imaginary scenes and covert response approximations again play a significant role. The flooding procedure usually involves repeated exposure to the feared situation through extensive and often exaggerated imagery. The key characteristic of this technique is prolonged exposure to the feared stimulus so that the person experiences stress and tension *without* the relief usually provided by escaping or avoiding the situation. (For this reason the procedure is sometimes called "response prevention.") Theoretically, the stress and tension responses gradually diminish, much as in an extinction procedure (Stampfl & Levis, 1967). Recent reviews (Baum, 1970; Morganstern, 1973) of the experimental literature on flooding have raised some questions about its therapeutic promise. Although "self-flooding" homework assignments have been given in some instances, formalized self-control treatment packages such as those in desensitization have not been reported. What with the crucial role of imagery and self-maintained arousal in flooding procedures, their adaptation to a self-regulated format would appear quite possible. However, such an adaptation must await the controlled demonstration of clinical utility on the part of the procedures themselves.

Several attempts have been made to change the cueing value of inappropriate covert responses. For example, Davison (1969) and Marquis (1970) have used a conditioning procedure designed to alter individuals' responses to deviant sexual images. In the case study reported by Davison, a young man successfully reduced the arousing capacities of sadistic sexual fantasies by pairing sexual cues of appropriate behavior (*Playboy* foldouts) with masturbation. The theoretical rationale involved is that the thoughts and images that occur just prior to orgasm (within a few seconds) may subsequently gain control over sexual arousal. By substituting appropriate cues for formerly maladaptive ones, the latter may lose their inappropriate cueing capacities. Marquis (1970) calls this process "orgasmic reconditioning" and reports several case studies that support its promise as a self-change strategy.

Working from a psychological as well as physiological perspective, Schultz and Luthe (1959) have developed a complex series of self-management procedures designed to amplify and alter covert response cues. These methods have been referred to as autogenic training and can be roughly described as a modern amalgam of self-hypnosis and yoga. In autogenic training, individuals are taught a series of relaxation procedures through hypnotic and focused attention procedures (e.g., attending to one's breathing, body temperature, etc.). Meditation skills are also developed in which visual and auditory hallucinations are encouraged and self-controlled. Studies conducted to date have suggested that a wide variety of covert events can be identified and altered through mastery of autogenic training exercises (Luthe, 1970). Unfortunately, most behavioral researchers have ignored autogenic training (along with self-hypnosis, yoga, and Zen), in part because the conceptual rationales involved have not comfortably fit into the orthodox framework of "behavior theory." The perspective advanced here advocates that *any* self-management technique that allows an individual to modify a relevant behavior should be considered empirically and clinically useful even if it does not fit into existing theoretical rationales.

The recent recommendation of Miller (1969) and his colleagues is relevant to this point. Miller has suggested that hypnotic behavior and some forms of focused attention may serve the same function in humans as do curare and other chemical agents in animals by facilitating voluntary control of certain physiological responses. Miller contends that a variety of glandular and visceral responses (e.g., asthma, headaches, blood pressure, etc.) can be voluntarily controlled, provided that training is given in the identification of private neurochemical events. Feedback on changes in these biological responses (i.e., "biofeedback") is needed to shape self-controlling skills. The close correspondence between the recommendations of Miller and the techniques used in autogenic training should be noted.

Several lines of evidence (Todd & Kelley, 1970; Barber *et al.*, 1971; Kamiya *et al.*, 1971; Sachs, 1971; DuPraw, 1972; Tart, 1972; Shapiro *et al.*, 1973) have supported the notion that focused attention, self-hypnosis, biofeedback, and autogenic training techniques offer much promise as self-controlling strategies. The scope of our present discussion prevents us from pursuing a more extensive review of the research in these areas, for their significance to self-control would merit a volume in itself. Conceptual eclecticism is necessary to wed these procedures to more conventional strategies, and expanding research efforts are needed to isolate and examine the processes involved in these self-regulatory performances.

COVERT RESPONSES AS TARGET BEHAVIORS

In the last section we discussed the identification of covert cues and methods for altering responses to those cues. Our present topic is actually an extension of this research. Given that one can identify the thoughts or images that contribute to a behavior problem, are there alternative means for producing change? Instead of altering one's response to private cues, can one rearrange the cues themselves to effect improvement? Using an internalized stimulus-control strategy, can one reduce the occurrence of problematical antecedents and increase the frequency of adaptive cognitive stimuli?

The modifiability of covert responses is an assumption that derives from the previously discussed correspondence between overt and covert behavioral processes. If it is true that private events are qualitatively and functionally similar to overt skeletal responses, then they too must be influenced by their antecedents and consequences. The validity of this continuity or homogeneity assumption was explored in a laboratory analogue by Mahoney, Thoresen, and Danaher (1972). Using a single-subject (ABAB) design, individuals were asked to memorize a series of noun pairs (e.g., "dog—bicycle") and to record what type of covert method they used for memorization (e.g., using the nouns in a sentence, creating a mental image of the two nouns interacting, or repeating the pairing over and over). First, subjects' baseline rates of using these methods were measured. Then, during the intervention phase, individuals were either rewarded with money or punished by withdrawal of money for using a specified covert associative method (e.g., imagery or repetition). In the subsequent reversal phase the target of this reward or punishment was altered. Finally, during the reintervention phase, the initial covert method again received either systematic reward or punishment. Data from this analogue experiment revealed that external contingencies produced highly predictable changes in subjects' covert responding: When imagery was rewarded, it increased; when it was punished, it decreased. To corroborate subjects' self-reports of covert behaviors, recall memorization of specific noun pairs was evaluated. Consistent with a wealth of evidence in human memory and learning (e.g., Paivio, 1969; Bower, 1970), recall was significantly better when imagery was reported as the covert associative method. These findings support the notion that covert events share many

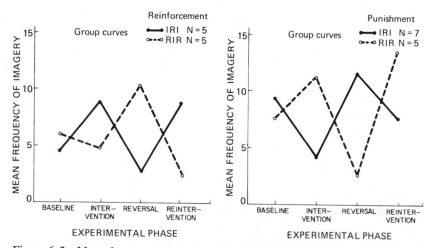

Figure 6–2   Mean frequency of imagery when subjects were alternately reinforced (*left*) for self-reports of imagery (IRI) or repetition (RIR), and (*right*) when alternately punished for self-reports of imagery or repetition. (Adapted from Mahoney, Thoresen, & Danaher, 1972. With the permission of Microform International Marketing Corporation, exclusive copyright licensee of Pergamon Press Journal back files.)

of the functional relationships known to exist with overt behaviors. They also suggest that private events can be studied, altered, and corroborated through controlled experimentation.

Many clinical instances of covert behavior modification have been mentioned in our previous discussion of other self-regulatory strategies. For example, Rutner and Bugle (1969) and Bucher and Fabricatore (1970) have reported successful elimination of hallucinations in hospitalized patients. Deviant sexual fantasies, obsessions, and depressive thoughts have likewise been altered (e.g., Mees, 1966a; Johnson, 1971; Mahoney, 1971; Jackson, 1972). Much of this work in covert self-control was stimulated by Homme's (1965) article on "coverants, the operants of the mind." Recognizing the significant role played by covert responses in behavior change, Homme recommended that behavioral engineers attend to their experimental analysis and modification. He outlined an exemplary technique for "coverant control," which utilized self-reward based on the Premack Principle. Using smoking as an illustrative target behavior, Homme suggested two therapeutic procedures: (1) the reduction of early response chain elements (i.e., urges to smoke) that lead to smoking, and (2) the increase of reinforcements for behaviors incompatible with smoking. The following coverant control sequence was recommended:

(1) Urge to Smoke $\rightarrow$	(2) Antismoking Thought (e.g., "Smoking causes cancer") $\rightarrow$	(3) Pro-Nonsmoking Thought (e.g., "My food will taste better") $\rightarrow$	(4) Reward (e.g., Coffee drinking)
HIGH-PROBABILITY BEHAVIOR $\rightarrow$	LOW-PROBABILITY BEHAVIOR $\rightarrow$	LOW-PROBABILITY BEHAVIOR $\rightarrow$	HIGH-PROBABILITY BEHAVIOR

Mahoney (1970) pointed out several potential problems in the above procedure and proposed some technical revisions. Although Homme's article stimulated many attempts to modify covert responses (e.g., Tooley & Pratt, 1967; Todd, 1972; Hannum, Thoresen, & Hubbard, 1974), few controlled experiments have been conducted on his recommended coverant control procedure.

Although a handful of studies (e.g., Rutner, 1967; Keutzer, 1968; Lawson & May, 1970; Tyler & Straughan, 1970; Gordon & Sachs, 1971) have reportedly used Homme's sequence, close examination reveals that they have either not specified the procedure employed or have modified the one proposed by Homme. A close approximation was reported by Horan and Johnson (1971), who asked overweight subjects to develop lists of negative thoughts about obesity and positive thoughts about not being overweight. Some were asked to repeat these coverant pairs to themselves several times a day, while others were told to reward them with a high probability behavior. After eight weeks only the latter group had lost a significant amount of weight as compared to a control group. The results are encouraging given the fact that only three brief counseling sessions were involved, and most subjects actually failed to carry out the treatment procedure.

The coverant strategy of Homme remains promising but as yet unsubstantiated by research. Erroneous extrapolations from Premackian theory have confounded many applications (see Chapter 4). However, there can be little doubt that Homme's impact on covert self-control has been both substantial and enduring. As we shall see, research evidence from other areas has supported his predictions regarding the behavior change potential of covert operants.

Meichenbaum and Cameron (1974), drawing upon the pioneering work of Luria (1961), Ellis (1962), Vygotsky (1962), Bem (1967), and O'Leary (1968), have recently reported a series of intriguing studies dealing with cognitive factors in behavior modification. In the training procedure that they developed, individuals are taught to self-monitor their "internal monologues" (i.e., what they say to themselves) in stress situations. For example, the speech-anxious student may find that he is engaging in a variety of self-arousing and counterproductive statements (e.g., "I know I'm going to blow this," "God, am I nervous!" etc.). In a formal training sequence, the individual is taught to change his covert self-instructions to more adaptive ones (e.g., "If I take my time and try to relax, I'll do alright," "I'm doing fine—nothing to worry about," etc.). These procedures have been applied to avoidance behaviors (e.g., animal phobias and test anxiety), creativity, impulsiveness, and schizophrenic "crazy talk" (Meichenbaum & Cameron, 1974). The findings of this research have consistently supported the therapeutic promise of "modifying what clients say to themselves."

Noteworthy in the Meichenbaum training procedure is the use of initial modeling, guided participation, and gradual shaping in the development of covert self-control. An illustrative sequence is as follows:

1. The therapist models adaptive self-cueing by talking out loud and administering task-relevant instructions to himself (e.g., "Relax, you're doing great; that's it.") as he performs the task.
2. The client is then asked to perform the task while the therapist instructs him aloud.
3. The client performs the task and instructs himself out loud.
4. The client performs the task and whispers instruction to himself.
5. The client performs the task and uses covert self-instructions.

This sequence is designed to parallel the internalization processes by which many self-cueing responses are acquired. Meichenbaum's rationale and methods are similar in many ways to Ellis' (1962) "rational-emotive therapy" and Lazarus' (1971b) "cognitive restructuring" techniques. Although this area is still relatively young, preliminary work has suggested that it has much to offer. The next decade of self-control research will undoubtedly witness a proliferation of these pioneering efforts.

The technique of "thought stopping" was developed by Wolpe (1958) for the termination of problematical covert responses. In this procedure, a client is asked to engage in the undesired thought or image and, when he has signalled that it is occurring, the therapist shouts the word "STOP!" In addition to startling the client, this procedure allegedly disrupts the problem behavior. The individual is subsequently trained to shout the word "STOP" first aloud and then to himself as a means of terminating undesired thoughts and images. Although Wolpe has reported clinical success with this strategy, little in the way of controlled research has been reported. Several investigators (e.g., Gershman, 1970; Yamagami, 1971) have indicated that thought stopping, usually in combination with other treatment procedures, has been helpful in individual therapy cases. In a comparative group study, Wisocki and Rooney (1971) found that thought stopping was equally as effective as covert sensitization (a procedure to be discussed shortly) in the reduction of smoking behavior. Generalizing from other research on covert self-control, one would not expect thought stopping to offer much promise as the sole treatment strategy for termination of problematical private events, for investigations with other techniques (e.g., Mahoney, 1971) have shown that the reduction of inappropriate covert responses does not automatically result in the increase of appropriate ones. This is consistent with the research reported in Chapters 4 and 5, suggesting that covert response patterns may often be relatively independent of one another. Reducing a person's self-criticism may not lead to increases in self-praise. By emphasizing only the negative aspect of behavior change, thought stopping delimits both its therapeutic scope and its probabilities for success. The simultaneous development of appropriate incompatible behaviors is highly desirable (Bandura, 1969).

The foregoing studies in this section have dealt with the modification of covert target behaviors, events that have considerable influence on other responses. Such interaction is demonstrated by the fact that, although some private events are aversive or undesirable in and of themselves (e.g., headaches, traumatizing memories), many become targets for change because of their relationship to subsequent maladaptive behaviors (e.g., suicide, avoidance responses, etc.).

The last two sections, relating to antecedents and target behaviors, have highlighted the complexity and continuity involved in covert self-control. A thought may represent an antecedent for subsequent performance and hence a target behavior for self-change. In the next section we shall pursue the continuum a bit further by discussing covert events as consequences.

COVERT RESPONSES
AS CONSEQUENCES

There is ample evidence to support the notion that positive and negative covert events can function in a way similar to overt reinforcers and punishers in the management of behavior. Weiner (1965), for example, has demonstrated that aversive consequences may have equivalent effects if they are simply imagined rather than actually experienced. The abundance of research on cognitive-symbolic processes has also shown that covert events play a significant role in moderating and modifying overt consequences (Dulany, 1968; Bandura, 1969; Staats, 1972). Anticipated consequences (i.e., images and thoughts about existing contingencies) are undoubtedly a major factor in complex human performance, a fact demonstrated in a study by Kaufman, Baron, and Kopp (1966). Subjects were told that they would be rewarded on various intermittent schedules. Individual performance data revealed that subjects responded at rates that were appropriate to the schedule they thought they were on rather than to the actual existing contingencies. Bandura (1971b) has noted the prevalence of misperceived contingencies in many forms of behavior pathology (e.g., compulsive rituals, paranoid delusions, etc.). When perceived contingencies are not readily corrected by "reality testing," they may continue to influence behavior for long periods of time.

Ferster, Nurnberger, and Levitt (1962) recognized that many self-regulatory problems were related to maladaptive consequence gradients, that is, immediately pleasant sensations (e.g., overeating) followed by very delayed aversive consequences. They recommended that individuals collapse time by imagining the ultimately aversive consequences of their actions early in the response chain. As we shall see, several formalized treatment strategies have incorporated this use of imaginary and anticipated consequences.

One of the earliest documented covert self-control techniques was that labeled "covert sensitization" by Cautela in 1966. Early studies utilizing this technique had a high success rate. The procedure was pioneered by Lazarus (1958), who asked a hypnotized client to imagine himself performing an undesired behavior (compulsive rituals) and experiencing aversive consequences (feelings of tension and uneasiness). The subject was then told to imagine terminating the behavior and feeling calm and relaxed (covert negative reinforcement). This method was reported as being successful in the elimination of the client's compulsive patterns. A similar case was reported by Miller (1959), who hypnotized an alcoholic patient and asked him to vividly re-experience his worst hangover, including the nausea, vomiting, and pain that accompanied it. The patient was conditioned to associate the smell and taste of alcoholic beverages with this aversive imagery. Clincal improvement was again reported. Several other early case histories (e.g., Gold & Neufeld, 1965; Kolvin, 1967) supported the therapeutic promise of this covert conditioning procedure.

In 1966, Cautela also outlined a formal treatment procedure for covert sensitization. The typical pattern requires the client, first, to be trained in deep muscular relaxation identical to that used in systematic desensitization. Imaginary conditioning scenes are then described by the therapist.

> You are sitting at your desk in the office preparing your lectures for class. There is a pack of cigarettes to your right. While you are writing, you put down your pencil and start to reach for the cigarettes. You get a nauseous feeling in your stomach. You begin to feel sick to your stomach, as if you are about to vomit. You touch the pack of cigarettes and bitter spit comes into your mouth. When you take the cigarette out of the pack some pieces of food come into your throat. Now you feel sick and have stomach cramps. As you are about to put the cigarette into your mouth, you puke all over the pack of cigarettes. The cigarette in your hand is very soggy and full of green vomit. There is a stink coming from the vomit. Snots are coming from your nose. Your hands feel all slimy and full of vomit. The whole desk is a mess. Your clothes are all full of puke. You get up from your desk and turn away from the vomit and cigarettes. You immediately begin to feel better being away from the vomit and cigarettes. You go to the bathroom and wash up and feel great being away from the vomit and the cigarettes (Cautela, 1971a, p. 113).

Cautela emphasizes two aspects of the use of such imagery. First, aversive stimuli (e.g., nauseous images) are paired with the problem behavior in a typical classical conditioning sense; that is, the conditioned and unconditioned stimuli are repeatedly associated with each other. Second, negative reinforcement or escape conditioning is involved. Observe, for example, that the smoker in the above sequence escaped from the nauseous smoking scene by leaving the situation and immediately feeling much better, suggesting that the avoidance of cigarettes will thereby be strengthened. Cautela, however, has not clearly acknowledged many of the specific processes and their theoretical relevance in the covert sensitization procedure. It seems quite clear that strict operant or classical conditioning rationales are both inadequate to explain the process (Rachman & Teasdale, 1969). Note, for instance, that in the above example a series of imaginal actions is immediately followed by a series of aversive images. The procedure is not a simple pairing of an unconditioned stimulus with escape conditioning added. The imaginal component is likewise preceded by having the person practice relaxation and by creating a strong expectancy that the technique works. In addition, the person can be said to be engaging in a type of self-modeling, visualizing himself in everyday life situations.

Covert sensitization has been the subject of a host of published case reports and studies (e.g., Cautela, 1966, 1967; Anant, 1967; Ashem & Donner, 1968; Barlow, Leitenberg, & Agras, 1969; Barlow, Agras, & Leitenberg, 1970; Sachs, Bean, & Morrow, 1970; Steffy, Meichenbaum, & Best, 1970; Wagner & Bragg, 1970; Wisocki, 1970; Gordon & Sachs, 1971; Wisocki & Rooney, 1971; Curtis & Presly, 1972; Manno & Marston, 1972). Nonetheless, few well-controlled studies have been conducted. The methodological problems discussed in Chapter 2 are particularly relevant to covert sensitization studies because, in using this procedure (1) several interventions are carried on concurrently as discussed above, (2) assessment of the onset, intensity, and duration of the average image is extremely difficult, and (3) other factors such as expectancy effects and demand characteristics of the situation may account for observed and self-reported changes.

In one of the first group experiments Ashem and Donner (1968), working with alcoholics, found that the sequence of scenes was irrelevant in producing change. Some subjects were asked, first, to imagine the problem situation (the conditioned stimulus situation) involving alcohol prior to imagining themselves feeling very nauseous and sick (the unconditioned stimulus situation). Other subjects, however, were asked to imagine the reverse sequence (i.e., nauseous scene before the problem situation). Both groups reported that they quickly associated and presumably intermixed the two on subsequent presentations. The study proved quite successful in helping almost half of the treated group remain abstinent from drinking at a six-month follow-up, compared with a no-contact control group.

The study is one of the few reported that attempted to examine the complexity of variables represented in a covert sensitization treatment. Commendably, the authors included a very specific statement of the treatment content for each of nine sessions. In their covert sensitization treatment each subject was first given training in deep muscular relaxation and assisted in constructing a hierarchy of problem-drinking situations. During later sessions, considerable time was spent on associating deep relaxation and feelings of calmness with visual images of pushing alcohol away, drinking nonalcoholic drinks, and engaging in behavior incompatible with drinking. Ashem and Donner reported that most subjects acquired a strong aversion to alcohol—the mere mention of the word or suggestion of a scene almost automatically induced a nauseous response. This anecdotal data provides further support for the arousal capacities of symbolic events.

Barlow, Leitenberg, and Agras (1969) reported an excellent controlled study of covert sensitization utilizing an intensive ABAB or treatment reversal design with a patient who was pedophilic (sexually attracted to very young girls). Results are shown in Figure 6–3. The contingent association of the aversive image with imagining the problem

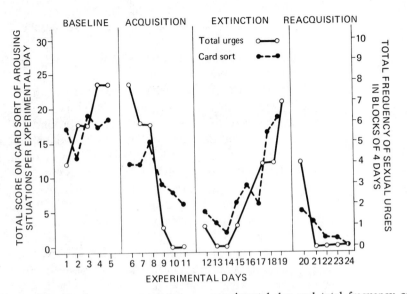

Figure 6–3   Total score on card sort per experimental day and total frequency of pedophilic sexual urges in blocks of four days surrounding each experimental day. Lower scores indicate less sexual arousal. (Adapted from D. H. Barlow, H. Leitenberg, & W. S. Agras, "Experimental Control of Sexual Deviation through Manipulation of the Noxious Scene in Covert Sensitization," *Journal of Abnormal Psychology*, 1969, 74, 599. Copyright 1969 by the American Psychological Association. Reprinted by permission.)

behavior during acquisition reduced the frequency of sexual urges and lowered the scores on a self-report measure of arousing situations. Findings indicated that imagining the problem situation without the aversive imagery (the extinction phase) actually *increased* urges and self-report scores. Baseline measurements were first taken, and, in the second (acquisition) phase, a sharp decelerating effect was produced that was dramatically reversed during the third (extinction) phase. The reintroduction of the aversive imagery, however, quickly diminished both measures during the final (reacquisition) phase.

In a subsequent study Barlow, Agras, and Leitenberg (1970) reported comparable findings for a male homosexual. They demonstrated that the expectancy effects could not explain the results, refuting critics of almost every reported covert sensitization study who postulated a positive correlation between the two conditions. Two male homosexual patients were given the expectancy that the covert sensitization procedure would probably increase the frequency of homosexual urges. However, they were assured not to be alarmed since the procedure was only being tried out for a short period. Using self-reported urges, self-ratings of problem situations, and penile blood volume as change measures while the subject was viewing color slides of male and female nude subjects, the authors demonstrated that covert sensitization still proved very effective despite the negative expectancy condition.

In a study dealing with smoking reduction (Wagner & Bragg, 1970), the treatment group found to be most successful combined systematic desensitization with covert sensitization. In this treatment, when the individual signaled anxiety while visualizing a situation in the usual systematic desensitization format, he was told to imagine himself picking up a cigarette and starting to light it; at this point the covert sensitization procedure was initiated. It is noteworthy that this combined treatment resulted in the most significantly maintained reduction in smoking. Subjects were given practice in not only associating smoking with an aversive event, but were also given practice imagining themselves *not* smoking in situations usually associated with that behavior. Such a combination fulfills the recommendation of Bandura (1969) and others—the efficacy of punishment techniques is typically enhanced when incompatible positive behaviors are also reinforced. Also, as will be noted later, this positive practice (imagining oneself not smoking) represents a vicarious self-modeling method.

Conclusions about the effectiveness of covert sensitization are complicated by (1) the lack of treatment standardization in terms of exposure time to the aversive image, (2) different types of imagery, (3) varying frequency and length of treatment sessions, ranging from almost daily to once a week for several weeks, (4) different amounts of out-of-office practice, and (5) the inclusion of group discussions and contingent therapist attention for improvement. Nonetheless, the data collected to date suggest that the association of an aversive image with an image of the target behavior can affect the frequency of an overt response. Variations of the standard covert sensitization procedure have also shown promise (e.g., Davison, 1968, 1969; Steffy, Meichenbaum, & Best, 1970; Berecz, 1972; Curtis & Presly, 1972; Manno & Marston, 1972). Further research is needed to identify the critical components in this strategy and to refine training techniques.

Exhausting the remaining types of covert consequences, Cautela (1969b, 1971a, 1971b) has described procedures involving four variations: (1) covert positive reinforcement, (2) covert negative reinforcement, (3) covert extinction, and (4) covert modeling. The first variation, covert positive reinforcement, involves the pairing of an imaged target behavior (e.g., an assertive response) with imaginary reinforcement (such as lying on a warm beach, winning a tennis match, etc.). Individualized reward scenes are developed and the client is trained to image one of these scenes to the word "reinforcement." Descriptions of appropriate responses are then followed by this command. In the second variation, covert negative reinforcement, an aversive scene (e.g., a painful injury) is imaged and then

replaced by an image of some desired behavior. Procedurally, this technique is more similar to covert "aversion relief" (Wolpe, 1958) than to negative reinforcement since the latter requires that a target behavior precede (rather than follow) termination of an aversive stimulus. The third variation, covert extinction, involves the symbolic enactment of a behavior with neutral imagined consequences. For example, a client who is anxious about stuttering might be asked to imagine himself beginning to stutter and being ignored. The fourth variation, covert modeling, as its name implies, requires that the person imagine observing others, as well as himself, performing an appropriate response. Note that since performance scenes are used in virtually all of the covert conditioning procedures, covert modeling must be considered a frequent element in these strategies (Kazdin, 1972).

Evidence for the effectiveness of covert conditioning is as yet very preliminary; complexity of design and concomitant difficulty of interpretation present some of the problems involved. Several case studies and a handful of laboratory experiments have been reported (e.g., Cautela, 1969a, 1970, 1971a, 1971b; Flannery, 1970; Wisocki, 1970; Ascher & Cautela, 1972; Cautela, Steffan, & Wish, in press). Unfortunately, most case studies involving covert conditioning have combined these procedures with other treatment techniques or have not controlled relevant experimental variables (e.g., client expectancies, therapist reinforcement, etc.).

Also, the group studies to date have lent some support to the notion that covert consequences can influence a range of overt responses (e.g., Ascher, 1971; Krop, Calhoon, & Verrier, 1971; Manno & Marston, 1972). However, the processes involved in these techniques have yet to be clarified. To what extent does covert self-modeling account for the effects observed? Does it matter whether the covert consequences follow symbolic representations or actual occurrences of a target behavior? Should the imagined consequences be realistic and relevant to the performance in question? These and other questions must await controlled investigations and clinical scrutiny.

COVERT SELF–CONTROL: PROBLEMS AND PROSPECTS

A wealth of theoretical and technical problems abound with covert self-control processes. In many ways we have consequences in search of conceptions. Many of the techniques described in this chapter appear to work in helping persons alter covert as well as overt actions, yet adequate conceptual rationales are lacking. Reliance on traditional conceptions such as classical conditioning or escape learning fail in a comprehensive manner to represent *all* of the overt as well as covert processes involved. The use of aversive imagery in covert sensitization, for example, is not readily explained simply by the pairing of two kinds of imagery responses with reference to escape or avoidance learning (Cautela, 1971a). Many other active ingredients operate in the clinical application of this technique, such as training in physical relaxation, establishing a strong positive expectancy, and the development of a goal-oriented hierarchy of performances. The potential relevance of vicarious processes in terms of observational learning has been often suggested in this chapter as an appropriate rationale. Many of the covert self-reinforcement and self-punishment procedures can be described as examples of vicarious self-modeling, wherein the person imagines himself engaging in certain behaviors and experiencing certain consequences in the presence of particular antecedent stimuli.

The primitiveness of theoretical rationales at present lends strong support to the need for an empirical approach as suggested by Figure 6–1. In this way overt and covert antecedents and consequences can be specified and either controlled or manipulated to assess results. An empircally based functionalism (Hilgard, 1969) would seem to be most appropriate at this juncture in minimizing any premature closure that might ignore possible variables of relevance. Much can be gained by exploring a broad spectrum of methods from cultural as well as theoretical perspectives, from alpha feedback to Zazen and Zen, as possible covert self-control techniques (cf., Barber *et al.*, 1971; Kamiya *et al.*, 1971; Shapiro *et al.*, 1973).

Much of the reported literature on covert techniques suffers from methodological and design problems. In Chapter 2 we suggested that data, if it is to be useful in expanding our knowledge of self-control phenomena, must be gathered under conditions that are publicly specifiable, testable, and replicable. The investigation of covert phenomena is complicated by the fact that the person himself has exclusive access to the data; hence, indirect methods are needed, which can partially substantiate data provided from self-reports. The relationship of certain external, observable behaviors that relate to covert responses should at some point be apparent. A person who has dramatically increased his positive evaluative self-thoughts should, for instance, demonstrate changes in certain external actions such as how he interacts with significant others. A chronic smoker who employs aversive imagery contingent upon urges to smoke should be observed to smoke less cigarettes.

Clearly, the study of covert processes used in a contingent fashion presents problems for which well-established scientific methods are still lacking (Tart, 1972). Yet many current standards of scientific inquiry can be applied without doing violence to the behavior under study. Most covert studies have failed to provide for such matters as (1) explicit definitions of techniques, (2) independent observations of other behaviors to substantiate self-report and to substantiate that the covert self-control techniques were used, (3) assessment of behavior to be controlled in the presence and absence of the self-control technique (by means of reversal, multiple baseline, or control group procedures), and (4) attention to problems of expectancy effects, experimenter or therapist bias, reactivity measurement effects, and bias in selecting subjects. While impressionistic clinical case studies can provide suggestive data, little can be learned from uncontrolled case studies about what processes actually produced change.

Information is needed to determine if many of the reported successes with covert techniques are simply a function of establishing strong expectancies for change coupled with direct suggestions and other demand characteristics necessary to participating in either an experiment or a controlled clinical study. An expectancy represents a possible covert response itself, a type of autosuggestion as in self-hypnosis that can bring about behavior change. Studies are needed to identify which covert processes, separately or in combination, are vital in producing specific changes in overt (and covert) behavior.

It is important to note that most of the well-controlled studies reviewed have been conducted in laboratory situations where little self-control was taking place (i.e., the experimenter controlled the situation). Hence, little evidence exists at present regarding the efficacy of many covert techniques when used by the person in everyday life situations. Further, evidence is scant that covert processes can be used to *maintain* behavior change over time periods exceeding a few weeks. A major research task therefore is to extend well-controlled experimental studies into everyday settings over long time periods.

One generalization stands out quite clearly: Effective covert self-control methods require careful environmental planning in which the person learns to self-manage by means of observation, practice, and direct feedback on performance. In this way a continuum is provided whereby the person gradually assumes more responsibility for the particular covert self-control technique. This generalization is highly consistent with the conception of self-control as a dynamic continuum of processes. Isolated covert techniques that fail to utilize the external environment in combination with covert and overt responses cannot provide the broad spectrum of actions that a person needs to alter his own behavior (especially those that are chronically well established). Therefore, the "best" covert techniques for self-control will probably be found in a combination of methods rather than any single procedure. Indeed, the presumably unitary techniques reviewed in this chapter are in fact a rich conglomeration of many overt procedures, that is, "treatment packages."

The covert techniques discussed in this chapter represent pioneering efforts in an exciting trend of therapy. These promising beginnings have much to offer empirically minded practitioners who are committed to creating ways of helping persons assume more responsibility for their own lives. Practitioners of many theoretical orientations have long been concerned with altering internal phenomena. The controlled empirical study of covert responses offers an exciting means of improving our understanding of such phenomena. In the next chapter we shall briefly consider the relevance of behavioral self-control for humanistic psychologists and educators.

Chapter

7

Summary and Implications

Self-control represents a dynamic continuum wherein the person alters the external environment as well as his own internal environment to promote meaningful change. Degrees of self-control exist: Sometimes the external environment arranged by others exercises considerable control over one's actions; at other times it is the individual who primarily influences what he does through self-managed cues and consequences. The paradigm of self-control presented here has minimized the long-standing traditional dichotomies such as internal versus external control and "self"-control versus environmental control. Such conceptions are anachronistic given what we now understand about human behavior. Clearly the exclusive inner-causation perspectives of many phenomenological orientations fail to account for the marked influence of external physical and social environments. Likewise, behavior conceptions that all but ignore the person's internal environment fall short by attributing all change to the external scene. The "in here" versus "out there" ways of thinking, lamented by Roszak (1969) and others, foster a conventional wisdom that has obstructed progress in solving the problems of self-control. Human behavior is no more the exclusive function of some hypothetical inner entity called willpower or self-actualizing drive than it is the sole consequence of external stimuli in the physical environment. Instead, human behavior is partly determined by internal or covert processes involving imaginal, subvocal, and physiological responses as well as by a variety of external events. Bandura (1969), after an extensive review of the literature, has suggested three major sources of regulation: stimulus control, symbolic covert control, and outcome control. These control mechanisms can function at a covert or internal level as well as externally. Such a conception is based on the homogeneity or continuity assumption that internal actions (viewed as responses) are susceptible to the same principles and hypotheses that have been demonstrated to influence overt behavior. Hence, stimulus control may occur through processes within the organism as well as without. In the same way, outcome control (consequences) may operate both within the person as well as externally. In this way, an *interdependent* perspective of self-control is offered whereby combinations of overt and covert events may function as antecedents, behaviors, and consequences.

The familiar equation $B=f(x)$ indicates that a specific behavior (B) can be controlled by arranging certain environmental conditions (x) (Goldiamond, 1965a). Such environmental conditions can be carried out by another person or by the individual himself. When the individual, however, arranges the environment, a second equation emerges: $x=f(B)$. The individual's environment (x) is a function (f) of his behavior (B). Thus the crucial interdependence of the individual acting on his environment and, in turn, being influenced by that environment—external as well as internal—is established. In this way, self-control is a function of internal and external environments and behaviors. The systems model (see Chapter 1) makes an important distinction between responses to be controlled (CR) and self-controlling actions (SCR). Self-control is behavior and like other human actions is mediated by symbolic or covert processes and ultimately maintained by external variables. One important consequence of making a clear distinction between behavior to be changed and self-controlling actions concerns the matter of the stability or maintenance of change. The self-controlling activities of an individual will not be carried on unless these actions are reinforced in some way and bring about positive change. Many efforts at self-change have floundered because of the failure to recognize this important distinction.

Given the notion of a broad continuum and an interdependence of covert and overt behaviors and environments, it is difficult to assess the criteria of what constitutes self-control. A working definition nonetheless has been proposed: An organism displays "self-control" when, in the relative absence of immediate external constraints, it engages in behavior whose previous probability has been less than that of alternatively available behavior (involving either less or delayed reward, greater exertion, or aversive properties, etc.). Further, self-control as a pattern of behavior relates directly to external controlling variables. This definition, in drawing upon Premack's (1965, 1971) probability rationale of reinforcement, highlights self-control as actions that have been relatively unlikely in previous situations.

Three major features are involved when self-control occurs: (1) two or more response alternatives exist, (2) the consequences of each alternative are usually conflicting, and (3) self-controlling actions are usually prompted and/or maintained by long-term *external* consequences. Obviously, if the person has no choice in a situation, he can exercise little self-control. In demonstrating self-control a decision between two or more alternatives must take place. The behavior to be increased, that is, the less likely behavior, involves consequences that are immediately less positive than the alternative "problem" behavior. A shy person, for example, may find initiating a conversation much less reinforcing than avoiding such situations. The systems model presented in Figure 1–1 (see Chapter 1) suggests that behavior to be managed (CR) is influenced by antecedent or initiating stimuli (AIS) as well as by consequences. Behavior may be increased (CR+), such as in making more positive responses to friends, or decreased (CR—), as in lowering food intake.

The probability of the behavior, that is, how often it will occur, can be altered by various kinds of self-controlling responses. Two basic strategies have been offered: *environmental planning* and *behavior programming*. Environmental planning essentially represents those actions that the individual takes to alter the situations preceding the target behavior. These "before the fact" activities can involve rearranging external stimulus cues and physical situations. Such changes are typically referred to as stimulus-control techniques. In addition, the person can prearrange for certain positive or negative consequences from others, contingent upon certain behaviors taking place. Internal cues can also be prearranged to "set the occasion" for a particular response. A husband, for instance, can rearrange his home environment to enable him to talk individually with each child by changing the seating arrangement at dinner. He can likewise arrange positive consequences for such conversations by asking his wife to compliment him on his conversations with each child. Finally, the father can engage in covert self-instructions just before sitting down to dinner as a way of cueing himself to talk with the children.

In contrast to environmental planning, behavioral programming takes place "after the fact" with the self-administration of consequences (overt and/or covert). The obese dieter can provide himself, for example, with a reward (anything but sweets, of course!) for evidence of some improvement in eating habits. Such a reward may be self-administered covertly (e.g., by conjuring up the "slim" image of himself at the beach) or overtly (e.g., by watching a favorite television program). Most of the clinical applications discussed in this book actually represent combinations of environmental planning and behavioral programming.

The expanded behavioral conception of self-control offered here is not limited by earlier notions that emphasized restraint and punishment. Instead, an unlimited spectrum of self-managed human action is possible within this paradigm. Further, the functional component analysis suggested by the model in Chapter 1 can include a rich combination of internal as well as external responses to foster self-control. The relevance of this richness for phenomenological and humanistic concerns has been repeatedly cited and will be discussed shortly. First, however, some of the methodological problems and issues are reviewed.

METHODOLOGICAL PROBLEMS

The need for more controlled research in the use of self-controlling techniques has been cited in every chapter. Some of the basic characteristics of scientific investigation, such as making procedures not only publicly specifiable and testable in an empirical fashion but also capable of replication, are much in need. The added complexity of covert actions coupled with external procedures, such as environmental planning, make it especially important to examine carefully the presumed relationship between technique and outcome. Too often the rival hypotheses of history, demand characteristics, expectancy effects, and bias in subject selection (cf. Campbell & Stanley, 1966) can readily account for reported changes. The use of positive self-reward of an external nature, as with a point or token economy system, may prove effective in large part because of many positive covert actions that concurrently take place within the person. When a strong positive expectation is created that a technique is really going to help, the person's problem behavior may be altered due to changes in covert self-instructions and positive self-thoughts rather than due to an external self-reward. Studies are needed that examine the interaction between overt and covert responses.

The problems of empirical assessment and evaluation are particularly difficult when the person is both assessor and assessee. Studies of self-observation have suggested that self-observation data, when compared with that of an external observor, often fail to show a high level of agreement (e.g., Herbert & Baer, 1972). Yet the effects of self-observation as a self-controlling technique are often reliable; that is, the behavior being observed demonstrates change. In most self-control work, the traditional scientific notion of a detached observer is difficult, especially when the behavior is internal. Indirect measures are required along with consensual validation through replications by trained observers (Tart, 1972). Concepts such as reactivity, observer agreement, and expectancy effect fail to fit comfortably as traditionally conceived in self-control investigations. A positive expectancy may, after all, actually represent certain covert responses, such as self-instructions or positive subvocalizations, and, as such, may be better thought of as self-controlling behavior rather than as a methodological inadequacy. Similarly, self-observation should be viewed in part as a therapeutically useful technique of self-control rather than as strictly a reactive measuring procedure (Kazdin, 1974). Nonetheless, the major tenets of controlled scientific inquiry are still much in need in self-control studies to reduce premature conclusions and faulty causal explanations. Independent observations, where possible, of the behavior to be controlled and the self-control technique should be utilized. The problems of independent confirmation are difficult but not impossible. A careful behavioral analysis of the situation can help considerably in clarifying which procedures are actually used and which consequences did, in fact, occur.

The conceptual confusions and inadequacies, especially those commented upon in Chapter 6, concerning covert techniques, deserve attention. At present, a variety of conceptual rationales has been used to "explain" self-control phenomena. Vicarious processes associated with modeling, for instance, have generally been ignored yet may provide a comprehensive theoretical rationale. Too often investigators have coined a new term to describe a phenomenon, thereby contributing to the theoretical confusion; the many ways of conceptualizing aversive imagery is but one of several examples (see Chapter 6). Attention to theoretical concepts and the ways they are employed to explain techniques will reduce some of the confusion and misapplications currently found in the literature. Many investigators, for example, failing to understand the theoretical work of Premack, have used inappropriate change techniques. A frequently occurring behavior is not necessarily a highly probable one in a reinforcing sense (see Chapter 4). At some point data must be gathered in ways that confirm or disprove the theoretical explanations. Self-control researchers and clinicians could help improve the present state of affairs by doing their conceptual homework more thoroughly.

In terms of self-controlling responses themselves, problems of maintenance and follow-through are crucial. Studies have demonstrated that immediate but transitory change can be brought about by almost any effort at self-control. The major task, however, is to develop techniques that allow the person to maintain and even accelerate positive change as time goes on. The maintenance problem remains an almost totally uninvestigated area. The systematic planning of environmental contacts in the form of "booster shots" offers one type of mechanism for maintenance (Patterson, 1973). Some type of combination of environmental planning and behavioral programming also seems very promising as a long-term solution to self-control. The individual must bring others into the picture in some way if the desired changes are to be maintained.

To date, then, the most promising self-control efforts have involved a mixture of self-observation, environmental planning, and behavioral programming (e.g., Mahoney, 1972b; Stuart & Davis, 1972). We simply do not know at this point the optimal combinations over time for individuals. This lack of knowledge suggests the need for empirical studies of treatment "packages" that combine various techniques with individuals across a variety of performance areas.

Additional problems with self-controlling actions involve (1) matters of the timing of self-control (i.e., before or after the behavior to be controlled), (2) the focus of self-control (i.e., the undesired behavior itself or a positive alternative), and (3) the unit of focus (i.e., relatively large chunks of behavior or small bits). The problems and issues involved represent a blend of practical as well as theoretical problems. These questions and issues will assume an even greater prominence as the range and variety of self-managed behavior expands.

OVERVIEW OF SELF–CONTROL TECHNIQUES

Self-Observation

The systematic gathering of information about one's own actions provides a basis for decisions about self-change. In addition, the process of self-observation (i.e., discriminating, counting, charting, and evaluating) can in itself often facilitate desired changes. Although theoretical approaches, both Eastern and Western, have stressed awareness and self-knowledge, the emphasis has usually been on gross discriminations. In contrast, behavioral self-observation stresses the detailed counting, charting, and evaluation of particular responses, either overt or covert. A growing number of studies has provided evidence that both the systematic counting and charting of certain actions are associated with positive changes in behavior. Further, individuals with brief training can learn to use self-observing devices such as wrist counters in everyday life settings to monitor internal and external actions. The use of a device for self-observation often becomes a discriminative cue that may exercise influence over the behavior being observed. A shy adolescent, for example, may find that a wrist counter used to record the number of times she engages in conversations with peers "reminds" her to start such conversations. The charting of self-observed data provides information on progress from which the person can make self-evaluations and engage in self-reward.

Controlled experimental studies of self-observation have only recently begun, thus leaving many important questions unanswered. Unfortunately, studies have too often confounded self-observation with other self-control and external techniques. Investigators now recognize self-observation as complex behavior in itself, which can serve not only as an assessment procedure but as a self-controlling technique. Limited evidence suggests that the self-observation of desirable responses may prove more effective than focusing on negative actions. A depressive patient, for example, may be helped by self-observing his positive thoughts more than by observing his depressive ruminations. In this way the person "accentuates the positive," thereby providing the basis for positive self-evaluation and self-reward. A related issue involves the timing and sequence of self-observation. "Earlier the better" may be a helpful motto in focusing on the antecedents of problem behaviors. In this way the chain of responses, often occurring in an automatic, nonconscious sense, may be disrupted sufficiently to modify the behavior in question. There is also the question of the size and magnitude of the behavioral unit to observe. Self-observation may become a burdensome task if too many behaviors are involved. Questions of how much, how often, and how many remain to be answered.

Self-observation, of course, does not take place in a vacuum but is related to a number of covert and overt processes. Its relation to self-reward has already been mentioned. In addition, the feedback value of self-observation, especially as regards specific goals or objectives, represents another important consideration. To date, the evidence is mixed as to whether explicit goal-setting facilitates the therapeutic effects of self-observation (Kolb, Winter, & Berlew, 1968; Mahoney, 1972b).

Self-observation in general seems to have an immediate but short-lived influence on behavior *unless* other self-controlling techniques are employed and/or unless the external environment changes in ways to support the desired behavior. One of the most pressing and practical issues in self-observation is that of developing training techniques to teach self-observation skills. The monitoring of covert events, such as specific thoughts and images, represents an especially important yet unexamined area of training.

Self-Reward

Positive self-reward, in which a person presents himself with a freely available positive reinforcer that is contingent upon his performing a certain action, has been the subject of a host of laboratory studies. Generally, self-award has been shown to be comparable in effectiveness to reinforcement that is externally administered. Laboratory studies by Kanfer as well as Bandura and their respective associates (see Chapter 4) have indicated that self-rewarding behavior can be trained either directly or vicariously through the use of social modeling. In general, the effects of self-reward are maximized when it is modeled by another person on a basis consistent with that expected of the observer. Rates of self-reward tend to parallel previous rates of external rewards; however, major discrepancies occur when the standard of performance increases and/or becomes ambiguous. Hence, self-reward practices are most effectively learned when the basis of self-evaluation is clear and consistent. From a self-management perspective, the self-administration of a reward in a situation whose criteria are determined by someone else should be differentiated from those situations in which the person himself determines the contingency and also administers the self-rewards. In some laboratory studies the contingencies have been externally controlled, thus limiting their relevance for self-reward in everyday situations.

Clearly, the role of self-evaluation is critical in understanding self-reward. One of the major obstacles in using self-reward as a self-control technique lies in the excessively high standards that many persons impose upon themselves. In this way, a person's performance is "never good enough" to merit self-reward. The combined use of external modeling, whereby others demonstrate realistic self-evaluation and reward, and covert modeling offers promise in facilitating more appropriate self-reward.

Unfortunately, controlled studies of negative self-reward, in which the person avoids or escapes from a freely avoidable aversive stimulus that is contingent on a certain performance, are lacking (cf. Penick, Filion, Fox, & Stunkard, 1971). The value of using positive and negative self-reward in combination seems particularly promising for reducing well-established negative behaviors (e.g., overeating, drinking, smoking).

Clinical studies have raised several questions that deserve exploration. Besides the many issues of type, intensity, and magnitude of reinforcing stimuli and schedules (e.g., continuous vs. intermittent), there is the question of current versus potential reinforcers. Is it more effective to use a new reinforcer, such as a long-awaited purchase or a special occasion, or a highly probable present response, such as a favorite television program or a cup of coffee? Based on Premack's (1965) reinforcement rationale, some type of self-denial or deprivation is required in the use of a highly probable behavior. The person in some way must deny himself drinking coffee or watching television if these actions are to be used contingently in self-reward. Without any disruption in the "natural" rate, a highly probable behavior cannot be used contingently. The self-denial aspect, of course, presents some self-management problems that deserve attention.

Although high-probability responses have been shown to be very promising as reinforcers, many studies to date have confused high-frequency behavior (e.g., urinating, opening a door) with highly probable behavior such as having a glass of beer or watching favorite shows on television. The clarification of high-frequency responses as stimulus cues that prompt behavior rather than as reinforcing consequences is one of the many problems that needs investigation.

Self-Punishment and Aversive Self-Regulation

The concepts of endurance (i.e., optionally remaining in an aversive situation) and restraint (i.e., optionally delaying or foregoing something positive) are best considered as controlled behaviors (CRs) rather than as self-controlling actions. To say that someone has exercised tremendous restraint does not identify which actions brought about this behavior. Laboratory studies indicate that persons who endure or restrain themselves are in fact using a variety of overt and covert self-controlling responses.

A person who self-administers aversive stimulation contingent upon some desirable behavior is utilizing negative self-punishment. Voluntarily removing positive stimuli after engaging in some undesirable behavior represents positive self-punishment. To qualify as a self-controlling action, self-punishment must be a self-imposed contingency wherein the person has control and the previous probability of aversive self-stimulation is taken into account. Many behaviors termed self-destructive are closely related to self-punishment but do not involve actions where the person is attempting to reduce an undesired behavior. Moreover, the immediate consequences of self-punitive or masochistic actions are often positive, thereby maintaining the behavior involved.

Unlike self-reward, the laboratory and the clinical literature on self-punishment is meager. Studies conducted to date suggest that self-punishment may be (1) acquired vicariously through observational experiences, (2) influenced by immediate consequences, and (3) somewhat independent of other methods of self-regulation, such as self-reward. Most of the clinical literature has focused on efforts, often unsuccessful, to reduce smoking and other chronic behaviors. Research has revealed great individual variability in both response to self-punishment and with failure to provide enduring change. Understandably, the "contract" or maintenance problem in the use of any self-imposed aversive experience is considerable because the person can, in fact, freely avoid the aversive stimuli. Thus the maintenance of self-change using aversive techniques is probably best managed when combined with some type of positive consequences for improvement.

Covert Self-Control

The continuity or homogeneity assumption argues that covert events, such as thoughts and images, have response status and, as such, are susceptible to the same generalizations and hypotheses found valid for external behavior. A variety of stimuli can be self-generated within the person to serve as self-controlling responses. Antecedents as well as consequences can occur within the individual separately or in combination with overt responses. Covert events may also represent behaviors to be controlled (CRs), such as hallucinations and negative self-thoughts. Although an impressive array of laboratory research (cf. Bandura, 1969) provides strong support for the continuity assumption, covert self-control methods remain obscure and relatively devoid of controlled research. A variety of theoretical rationales has been used to explain a large number of covert methods. However, careful examination of the actual processes reveals that simple conditioning rationales have generally failed to account for the phenomena involved. Because of the prevalence of imaginal cues, performances, and consequences in all covert self-control techniques, there is some reason to believe that symbolic, vicarious learning processes (e.g., modeling) are extensively involved.

It is important also to note the overlap of covert self-control with techniques of self-reward and self-punishment. The covert sensitization procedure, for instance, is an obvious example of negative self-punishment coupled with other external techniques. Most covert techniques involve more than the contingent use of a particular covert response. Typically, relaxation training, instructions, positive suggestion, and outside "homework" assignments are involved. Hence covert self-control involves a mixture of covert and overt procedures, some self-administered and some controlled by others. The most successful covert methods have involved well-structured initial training wherein control was externally administered by the experimenter or therapist and gradually given to the person. Further, there appears to be very limited value in the exclusive use of covert responses for self-control without some kind of concurrent environmental support.

The methodological problems of examining covert processes are considerable but not insurmountable. Attention to some basic characteristics of scientific research (see Chapter 2) will greatly enhance the usefulness of data currently being provided. At present, the most pressing need involves experimental refinement through controlled intensive experiments and factorial group studies. Particularly promising have been efforts (e.g., Suinn & Richardson, 1971; Meichenbaum & Cameron, 1974) to develop training systems for covert self-control. In addition a number of Eastern and "nonbehavioral" covert methods (e.g., meditation) offer considerable promise and are deserving of careful empirical examination.

BEHAVIORAL HUMANISM

A variety of humanisms have existed since the time of Hellenic civilization; at present there are classical, ethical, scientific, religious, Christian, and rational humanists. A blending of these is often referred to as humanistic psychology (cf. Buhler & Allen, 1972). A major theme of most humanists has been the concern that the individual person assume full responsibility for his own actions; what he experiences in life is seen as a function of who he is and what he does. Although the humanistic position is often contrasted with that of behaviorism (e.g., Skinner, 1971), we believe that behavioral self-control offers a valuable means for promoting humanistic ends. The recent award to B. F. Skinner as Humanist of the Year (1972) by the American Humanist Association denotes the overlap between the two perspectives. A thorough discussion of the relationship between behavioral psychology and contemporary humanism (i.e., humanistic psychology and education) has been presented elsewhere (Thoresen, 1973a).

Maslow (1969), the founder of humanistic psychology, once observed that the first and foremost task is "to *make* the Good Person." Indeed, the notion of creating the good person permeates humanistic literature. Humanistic psychologists and educators are particularly concerned about helping the person (1) experience life in a more integrated and harmonious fashion, (2) extend awareness, especially of internal behavior, in order to reduce the automaticity of actions, (3) act more compassionately with others and communicate in more personal and intimate ways, (4) make one's own personal decisions, being conscious of the meaning and values of certain actions, and (5) transcend or move beyond the immediate environment and its influence. These concerns *conceptualized as human actions* can be encouraged if the appropriate kinds of environmental experiences are arranged in order for learning to take place. Elements of the wide array of "humanistic" experiences now advocated (cf. Gustaitis, 1969), such as encounter groups, drugs, meditation exercises, sensory training, and yoga, have promise for promoting certain behaviors. However, the strong "militant rhetoric of anti-rigor" (Koch, 1969), that is, the antiscientific position manifested by many humanists, has seriously limited understanding of the processes involved in such experiences. There are, of course, a variety of ways to help individuals increase certain "humanistic" behaviors. The techniques of self-reward, self-punishment, covert self-control, and environmental planning can clearly be used to encourage humanistic actions. Indeed, a closer examination of many encounter/awareness/sensory experiences indicates that variations of these strategies are frequently employed for personal growth and development.

Many Eastern techniques, such as various forms of yoga and Zen, have been advocated by humanists because of their integrating focus and strong emphasis on internal actions. Transcendental meditation (cf. Wallace, 1970)and Zazen or Zen meditation (cf. Lesh, 1970) are two examples of self-control techniques that can be readily conceptualized in a social learning framework. In these covert self-control techniques the person utilizes a quiet physical environment and particular actions, such as breathing or the repetition of a mantra, or subvocalization (e.g., "Hari Om"). The consequences of these covert techniques, which often employ positive imagery responses and covert self-instructions, involve reduced physiological activity (e.g., reduced oxygen consumption and heart rate). In addition, the experience of deep calmness and relaxation is often reported by persons. With repeated practice, thought management does occur, for individuals report a reduction in "worries" and troublesome thoughts. It is important to note that a procedure such as transcendental meditation represents a series of self-controlling responses. In training, much use is made of positive suggestions and expectancies, along with external modeling and reinforcement for practice. "Homework" assignments, such as practicing twice daily for thirty minutes, are common. Interestingly, Boudreau (1972) recently reported a successful case in which a college student used transcendental meditation to eliminate a variety of claustrophobic behaviors. A hierarchy of problem situations was used with the client meditating after imagining the phobic scenes. Unfortunately, specific information on treatment was not provided in the article. The same study reported a second successful case in which yoga, presumably involving various physical movements (Hatha Yoga), was used daily, after symbolic systematic desensitization had failed to reduce the client's excessive perspiring in everyday situations (e.g., the classroom).

Many of the humanistically oriented techniques used in various kinds of group environments, however, fail to provide self-controlling skills. Too often the focus is excessively insightful rather than "outsightful." That is, the person focuses on historical understandings and current interpretations rather than on the functional relationship between his own behavior and the immediate environment (Ferster, 1972). A major problem with humanistic procedures is their heavy emphasis on what might be referred to as discrimination and arousal. In terms of physical and social environments, the person is often provided with very powerful experiences, which elicit strong responses. These arousing stimuli are geared to break or disrupt a person's set or frame of reference, "to blast a person out of his mind—sets and frames of reference—into a broader awareness" (Gustaitis, 1969, p. 79). Such experiences undoubtedly may "turn on" the person who may be powerfully stimulated to change; however, the person may not have in his repertoire the self-controlling skills needed to enact new behaviors and maintain them in everyday life situations (Liberman, 1972).

The intersection of social learning and humanistic approaches is perhaps best reflected in the recent development of transpersonal psychology—a movement started by Abraham Maslow in the late 1960s (cf. Sutich, 1969). Transpersonal approaches are aimed at expanding the *personal boundaries* of individuals to facilitate what is termed "mind and body self-control." Processes such as Zen, yoga, hypnosis, autogenic training, biofeedback, and meditation are advocated; in fact, any technique that enhances greater personal self-control may be used. The techniques of behavioral self-control are obviously relevant as means for helping the person expand the range of self-mastery; further "transpersonal techniques" are *not* a distinct new approach as contended (Astor, 1972) but share many things in common with the behavioral strategies presented here. The concept of the "transpersonal" is in many ways isomorphic with the social learning perspective of behavioral self-control.

Perhaps a major distinction to date between humanistic-transpersonal and behavioral efforts has been the type of human actions receiving attention. Behaviorally oriented psychologists have been typically struggling with chronic negative behaviors, such as alcoholism, obesity, and smoking. By contrast, humanistic psychologists have worked with persons concerned with increasing their positive actions with no immediate problem existing —at least immediate in requiring prompt attention.

Questions of personal meaning, purpose, awareness, and experiencing have generally dominated the concerns of humanists. Yet these same

concerns are of interest to behavioral investigators (e.g., Kanfer & Phillips, 1970; Staats, 1972; Thoresen, 1973a), for questions of perceived locus of control and personal attribution (i.e., thoughts of what causes one's actions) do relate to self-control. A person's sense of purpose and meaning is in part a function of whether he sees his actions as under his own control. Does the person, for example, label his covert experiences (in terms of thoughts, physiological reactions, and imagery responses) in positive, self-enhancing terms or in negative self-critical ways? One way of viewing intentionality (May, 1969) is in terms of certain covert images and self-statements. These covert responses interact to provide what is sometimes called "personal meaning." Indeed, as we observed in Chapter 6, meaning may emerge from the use of certain words as conditioned discriminative cues and as reinforcing stimuli in particular life situations. Certain words and images can be associated systematically by the individual with other words and images as well as overt experiences to create new personal meaning (cf. Staats, 1972).

May (1969), in speaking of the crisis of will, discusses the individual's feeling of powerlessness. The concept of will, according to May, is the capacity to organize one's self so that movement in a certain direction or towards a certain goal may take place. The lack of this capacity understandably leads to a sense of futility and despair. The techniques of behavior self-control reviewed here offer much in providing persons with this capacity to organize and move in desired directions. Conceptualizing self-control as a complex of actions (overt and covert) rather than as some inner force or entity, however, is essential in advancing our understanding of self-regulatory phenomena.

The key to self-mastery is not to be found in appeals to willpower and other presumed inner resources, but rather in awareness, *the knowledge of how to use various stimuli to increase and decrease certain responses*. In effect, the person who learns how to manipulate his own sources of stimuli by arranging his internal as well as external environments is one who exhibits self-mastery. It is now possible to "control the uncontrollable"—the internal environment (cf. Hefferline & Bruno, 1971). If the skills of behavioral self-control are to foster positive self-enhancing behaviors, we must move away from the rhetoric that divides and toward a personal empiricism that synthesizes.

THERAPY AS SELF–CONTROL TRAINING

A major contribution of behavioral approaches to therapy has been the emphasis on teaching and learning, viewing therapy as an educational process in which the client is assisted in learning more appropriate behaviors (Thoresen & Hosford, 1973). Although this teaching–learning paradigm has been a fruitful one, the structure has emphasized external control. The counselor or therapist has played the major role in carrying out behavioral assessments, diagnoses, and treatment. Too often the results have been short-lived, for positive behavior change has faded as contact with the counselor has diminished (e.g., Patterson, 1973). A major implication of work in behavioral self-control is that one should view counseling and therapy as training grounds for the development of self-control skills. Kanfer (1973) and others have signaled the need to shift control from the therapist to the person himself. "Instigation therapy" refers to those cases in which the therapist promotes behavior change through self-regulation in the natural environment (Kanfer & Phillips, 1966). One way to accomplish this shift is to increase the preventive and social thrust of self-control efforts. This increase can be accomplished by teaching behavioral self-control to social groups, such as school classes and parent organizations. In this way, many persons can learn the basic skills of environmental planning and behavioral programming to use not only in solving problems, but possibly in preventing major problems from developing. Different types of courses, seminars, and workshops in behavioral self-management should be developed and offered widely. The local adult education setting, for example, is one that could reach a large number of parents and adults. Hence a major task of counselors would be in organizing and presenting courses and workshops in self-control. Such training will require a large number of empirical studies on effective and efficient training methods. The task of training has found a promising beginning in the work of Suinn and Richardson (1971) and Meichenbaum and Cameron (1974).

The need for massive self-control training in education has recently been acknowledged (Glaser, 1972). Children should be taught a variety of self-management skills in such a way that they can modify their own environments for their own learning requirements. Individualized learning systems would thereby-be enhanced greatly since such programs often require a considerable amount of self-management. The same rationale holds for clients in general; they should be taught the skills of behavioral self-control so that they can control environments.

PERSONAL FREEDOM

The individual who knows the many environments (including his own internal one) that influence him and who manages them in order to enhance certain actions consistent with personal values is manifesting considerable dignity. We have suggested that behavior is not only a function of environment, but environments themselves are a function of the individual's behavior. Thus,

> . . . the truly "free" individual is one who is in intimate contact with himself and his environment (both internal and external). He knows "where he's at" in terms of the factors influencing both his actions and his surroundings. Moreover, he has acquired technical skills which enable him to take an active role in his own growth and adjustment. He is no mechanical automaton, passively responding to environmental forces. He is a personal scientist, a skilled engineer capable of investigating and altering the determinants of his actions. (Mahoney & Thoresen, 1974)

Behavioral self-control skills, although rudimentary at present, hold great promise as a means of giving "power to the person." The decade of the 1970s will hopefully see a careful expansion of this empirical humanism.

References

Allen, M. K., & Liebert, R. M. Children's adoption of self-reward patterns: Model's prior experience and incentive for non-imitation. *Child Development*, 1969, *40*, 921–926. (a)

Allen, M. K., & Liebert, R. M. Effects of live and symbolic deviant-modeling cues on adoption of a previously learned standard. *Journal of Personality and Social Psychology*, 1969, *11*, 253–260. (b)

Anant, S. S. A note on the treatment of alcoholics by a verbal aversion technique. *Canadian Psychologist*, 1967, *8*, 19–22.

Aronfreed, J. The origin of self-criticism. *Psychological Review*, 1964, *71*, 193–217.

Aronfreed, J. *Conduct and conscience: The socialization of internalized control over behavior.* New York: Academic Press, 1968.

Ascher, M. An analogue study of covert positive reinforcement. Paper presented at the Fifth Annual Meeting of the Association for the Advancement of Behavior Therapy, Washington, D.C., September 1971.

Ascher, M., & Cautela, J. R. Covert negative reinforcement: An experimental test. *Journal of Behavior Therapy and Experimental Psychiatry*, 1972, *3*, 1–5.

Ashem, B., & Donner, L. Covert sensitization with alcoholics: A controlled replication. *Behaviour Research and Therapy*, 1968, *6*, 7–12.

Astor, M. H. Transpersonal approaches to counseling. *Personnel and Guidance Journal*, 1972, *50*, 801–808.

Axelrod, S., Hall, R. V., Weis, L., & Rohrer, S. Use of self-imposed contingencies to reduce the frequency of smoking behavior. In M. J. Mahoney & C. E. Thoresen, *Self-control: Power to the person.* Monterey, Calif.: Brooks-Cole, 1974.

Azrin, N. H., & Powell, J. Behavioral engineering: The reduction of smoking behavior by a conditioning apparatus and procedure. *Journal of Applied Behavior Analysis*, 1968, *1*, 193–200.

Azrin, N. H., & Powell, J. Behavioral engineering: The use of response priming to improve prescribed self-medication. *Journal of Applied Behavior Analysis*, 1969, *2*, 39–42.

Bandura, A. *Principles of behavior modification.* New York: Holt, Rinehart and Winston, Inc., 1969.

Bandura, A. *Social learning theory.* New York: General Learning Press, 1971. (a)

Bandura, A. Vicarious and self-reinforcement process. In R. Glaser (Ed.), *The nature of reinforcement.* New York: Academic Press, 1971. Pp. 228–278. (b)

Bandura, A., Grusec, J. E., & Menlove, F. L. Some social determinants of self-monitoring reinforcement systems. *Journal of Personality and Social Psychology*, 1967, *5*, 449–455.

Bandura, A., & Kupers, C. J. Transmission of patterns of self-reinforcement through modeling. *Journal of Abnormal and Social Psychology*, 1964, *69*, 1–9.

Bandura, A., & Mahoney, M. J. Maintenance and transfer of self-reinforcement functions. Unpublished manuscript, Stanford University, 1973.

Bandura, A., & Mischel, W. Modification of self-imposed delay of reward through exposure to live and symbolic models. *Journal of Personality and Social Psychology*, 1965, *2*, 698–705.

Bandura, A., & Perloff, B. Relative efficacy of self-monitored and externally imposed reinforcement systems. *Journal of Personality and Social Psychology*, 1967, *7*, 111–116.

Bandura, A., & Walters, R. H. *Social learning and personality development.* New York: Holt, Rinehart and Winston, Inc., 1963.

Bandura, A., & Whalen, C. K. The influence of antecedent reinforcement and divergent modeling cues on patterns of self-reward. *Journal of Personality and Social Psychology*, 1966, *3*, 373–382.

Barber, T. X., DiCara, L. V., Kamiya, J., Miller, N. E., Shapiro, D., & Stoyva, J. (Eds.), *Biofeedback and self-control.* Chicago: Aldine-Atherton, 1971.

Barber, T. X., & Hahn, K. W., Jr. Experimental studies in "hypnotic" behavior: Physiological and subjective effects of imagined pain. *Journal of Nervous and Mental Disease*, 1964, *139*, 416–425.

Barlow, D. H., Agras, W. S., & Leitenberg, H. Experimental investigations in the use of covert sensitization in the modification of sexual behavior. In R. W. Rubin and C. M. Franks (Eds.), *Advances in behavior therapy*, Vol. 3. New York: Academic Press, 1970.

Barlow, D. H., Leitenberg, H., & Agras, W. S. Experimental control of sexual deviation through manipulation of the noxious scene in covert sensitization. *Journal of Abnormal Psychology*, 1969, *74*, 596–601.

Bass, B. A. Demand characteristics as a determinant of self-reinforcement. Unpublished doctoral dissertation, University of Tennessee, 1971.

Baum, M. Extinction of avoidance responding through response prevention (flooding). *Psychological Bulletin*, 1970, *74*, 276–284.

Bem, D. Self-perception theory. In L. Berkowitz (Ed.), *Advances in experimental social psychology*, Vol. 6. New York: Academic Press, 1972. Pp. 1–62.

Bem, S. L. Verbal self-control: The establishment of effective self-instructions. *Journal of Experimental Psychology*, 1967, *74*, 485–491.

Beneke, W. M., & Harris, M. B. Teaching self-control of study behavior. *Behaviour Research and Therapy*, 1972, *10*, 35–41.

Berecz, J. Modification of smoking behavior through self-administered punishment of imagined behavior: A new approach to aversion therapy. *Journal of Consulting and Clinical Psychology*, 1972, *38*, 244–250.

Bergin, A. R. A self-regulation technique for impulse control disorders. *Psychotherapy: Theory, Research and Practice*, 1969, *6*, 113–118.

Bernard, H. S., & Efran, J. S. Eliminating versus reducing smoking using pocket timers. *Behaviour Research and Therapy*, 1972, *10*, 399–401.

Bernstein, D. A. Modification of smoking behavior: An evaluative review. *Psychological Bulletin*, 1969, *71*, 418–440.

Bernstein, D. A. The modification of smoking behavior: A search for effective variables. *Behaviour Research and Therapy*, 1970, *8*, 133–146.

Bijou, S. W., Peterson, R. F., & Ault, M. F. A method of integrating descriptive and experimental field studies at the level of data and empirical concepts. *Journal of Applied Behavior Analysis*, 1968, *1*, 175–191.

Blackburn, T. Sensuous-intellectual complementarity in science. *Science*, 1971, *172*, 1003–1007.

Bolstad, O. D., & Johnson, S. M. Self-regulation in the modification of disruptive classroom behavior. *Journal of Applied Behavior Analysis*, 1972, *5*(4), 443–454.

Boudin, H. M. Contingency contracting as a therapeutic tool in the deceleration of amphetamine use. *Behavior Therapy*, 1972, *3*, 604–608.

Boudreau, L. Transcendental meditation and yoga as reciprocal inhibitors. *Journal of Behavior Therapy and Experimental Psychiatry*, 1972, *3*, 47–78.

Bower, G. Imagery as a relational organizer in associative learning. *Journal of Verbal Learning and Verbal Behavior*, 1970, *9*, 529–533.

Bower, G. Mental imagery and associate learning. In L. Gregg (Ed.), *Cognition and learning in memory*. New York: Wiley, 1972.

Boyd, N. S., & Sisney, V. V. Immediate self-image confrontation and changes in self-concept. *Journal of Consulting and Clinical Psychology*, 1967, *31*, 291–294.

Bridger, W. H., & Mandel, I. J. A comparison of GSR fear responses produced by threat and electric shock. *Journal of Psychiatric Research*, 1964, *2*, 278–282.

Bridgman, P. W. *The way things are*. Cambridge, Mass.: Harvard University Press, 1959.

Brigham, T. A., & Bushell, D. Notes on autonomous environments: Student-selected versus teacher-selected rewards. Unpublished manuscript, University of Kansas, 1972.

Brigham, T. A., & Sherman, J. A. Effects of choice and immediacy of reinforcement on single response and switching behavior of children. *Journal of the Experimental Analysis of Behavior*, in press.

Broden, M., Hall, R. V., & Mitts, B. The effect of self-recording on the classroom behavior of two eighth-grade students. *Journal of Applied Behavior Analysis*, 1971, *4*, 191–199.

Browning, R. M., & Stover, D. O. *Behavior modification in child treatment: An experimental and clinical approach.* Chicago: Aldine-Atherton, 1971.

Bucher, B., & Fabricatore, J. Use of patient-administered shock to suppress hallucinations. *Behavior Therapy*, 1970, *1*, 382–385.

Buhler, C. Basic theoretical concepts of humanistic psychology. *American Psychologist*, 1971, *26*, 378–386.

Buhler, C., & Allen, M. *Introduction to humanistic psychology.* Monterey, Calif.: Brooks-Cole, 1972.

Campbell, D. T., & Stanley, J. C. *Experimental and quasi-experimental designs for research.* Chicago: Rand McNally, 1966.

Carnegie, D. *How to stop worrying and start living.* New York: Simon & Schuster, 1948.

Catania, A. C. The pigeon's preference for free choice over forced choice. Paper presented to the Psychonomic Society, St. Louis, November 1972.

Cautela, J. R. Treatment of compulsive behavior by covert sensitization. *Psychological Record*, 1966, *16*, 33–41.

Cautela, J. R. Covert sensitization. *Psychological Reports*, 1967, *20*, 459–468.

Cautela, J. R. Behavior therapy and self-control: Techniques and implications. In C. Franks (Ed.), *Behavior therapy: Appraisal and status.* New York: McGraw-Hill, 1969. Pp. 323–340. (a)

Cautela, J. R. The use of imagery in behavior modification. Paper presented to the Annual Meeting of the Association for the Advancement of Behavior Therapy, Washington, D.C., September 1969. (b)

Cautela, J. R. Covert negative reinforcement. *Journal of Behavior Therapy and Experimental Psychiatry*, 1970, *1*, 273–278.

Cautela, J. R. Covert conditioning. In A. Jacobs and L. B. Sachs (Eds.), *The psychology of private events: Perspective on covert response systems.* New York: Academic Press, 1971. Pp. 109–130. (a)

Cautela, J. R. Covert extinction. *Behavior Therapy*, 1971, *2*, 192–200. (b)

Cautela, J. R. Covert modeling. Paper presented at the Fifth Annual Meeting of the Association for the Advancement of Behavior Therapy, Washington, D.C., September 1971. (c)

Cautela, J. R., Steffan, J., & Wish, P. An experimental test of covert reinforcement. *Journal of Consulting and Clinical Psychology*, in press.

Chapman, R. F., Smith, J. W., & Layden, T. A. Elimination of cigarette smoking by punishment and self-management training. *Behaviour Research and Therapy*, 1971, *9*, 255–264.

Chassan, J. B. *Research design in clinical psychology and psychiatry*. New York: Appleton, 1967.

Chein, I. *The science of behavior and the image of man*. New York: Basic Books, 1972.

Colle, H. A., & Bee, H. L. The effects of competence and social class on degree of modeling of self-reward patterns. *Psychonomic Science*, 1968, *10*, 231–232.

Curtis, R. H., & Presly, A. S. The extinction of homosexual behavior by covert sensitization: A case study. *Behaviour Research and Therapy*, 1972, *10*, 81–83.

Danaher, B. G. The theoretical foundations and clinical applications of the Premack principle: A review and critique. *Behavior Therapy*, in press.

Davison, G. C. Elimination of a sadistic fantasy by a client-controlled counter conditioning technique: A case study. *Journal of Abnormal Psychology*, 1968, *73*, 84–89.

Davison, G. C. Self-control through "imaginal aversive contingency" and "one-downmanship": Enabling the powerless to accommodate unreasonableness. In J. D. Krumboltz & C. E. Thoresen (Eds.), *Behavioral counseling: Cases and techniques*. New York: Holt, Rinehart and Winston, Inc., 1969. Pp. 319–327.

Davison, G. C. Counter-control in behavior modification. In L. A. Hamerlynck, L. C. Handy, & E. J. Mash (Eds.), *Behavior change: Methodology, concepts, and practice*. Champaign, Ill.: Research Press, 1973. Pp. 153–167.

Day, W. F. Methodological problems in the analysis of behavior controlled by private events: Some unusual recommendations. Paper presented at the Seventy-ninth American Psychological Association meeting, Washington, D.C., 1971.

deChardin, P. T. *The phenomenon of man*. New York: Harper & Row, 1959.

Donner, L. Automated group desensitization—a follow-up report. *Behaviour Research and Therapy*, 1970, *8*, 241–247.

Dorsey, T. E., Kanfer, F. H., & Duerfeldt, P. H. Task difficulty and noncontingent reinforcement schedules as factors in self-reinforcement. *Journal of General Psychology*, 1971, *84*, 323–334.

Dulany, D. E. Awareness, rules, and propositional control: A confrontation with S-R behavior theory. In T. R. Dixon & D. L. Horton (Eds.), *Verbal behavior and general behavior theory*. Englewood Cliffs, N.J.: Prentice-Hall, 1968, Pp. 340–387.

DuPraw, V. Self-management of internal responses: Heart-rate control. Unpublished doctoral dissertation, Stanford University, 1972.

D'Zurilla, T. Reducing heterosexual anxiety. In J. D. Krumboltz & C. E. Thoresen (Eds.), *Behavioral counseling: Cases and techniques*. New York: Holt, Rinehart and Winston, Inc., 1969. Pp. 442–454.

Elliott, R., & Tighe, T. Breaking the cigarette habit: Effects of a technique involving threatened loss of money. *Psychological Record*, 1968, *18*, 503–513.

Ellis, A. *Reason and emotion in psychotherapy.* New York: Stuart, 1962.

Ferster, C. B. Classification of behavior pathology. In L. Krasner & L. P. Ullmann (Eds.), *Research in behavior modification.* New York: Holt, Rinehart and Winston, Inc., 1965. Pp. 6–26.

Ferster, C. B. An experimental analysis of clinical phenomena. *Psychological Record*, 1972 (Winter), *22*(1), 1–16.

Ferster, C. B., Nurnberger, J. I., & Levitt, E. B. The control of eating. *Journal of Mathetics*, 1962, *1*, 87–109.

Ferster, C. B., & Skinner, B. F. *Schedules of reinforcement.* New York: Appleton, 1957.

Fixsen, D. L., Phillips, E. L., & Wolf, M. M. Achievement place: The reliability of self-reporting and peer-reporting and their effects on behavior. *Journal of Applied Behavior Analysis*, 1972, *5*, 19–30.

Flannery, R. The investigation of differential effectiveness of office vs. *in vivo* therapy of a simple phobia: An outcome study. Unpublished doctoral dissertation, University of Windsor, 1970.

Flowers, J. V. Behavior modification of cheating in an elementary school student: A brief note. *Behavior Therapy*, 1972, *3*, 311–312.

Flowers, J., & Marston, A. Modification of low-self-confidence in elementary school children. *Journal of Educational Research*, in press.

Fox, L. Effecting the use of efficient study habits. *Journal of Mathetics*, 1962, *1*, 76–86.

Frank, J. *Persuasion and healing; a comparative study of psychotherapy.* Baltimore, Md.: Johns Hopkins Press, 1961.

Gershman, L. Case conference: Transvestite fantasy treated by thought-stopping, covert sensitization and aversive shock. *Journal of Behavior Therapy and Experimental Psychiatry*, 1970, *1*, 153–161.

Gewirtz, J. L. The roles of overt responding and extrinsic reinforcement in "self-" and "vicarious-reinforcement" phenomena and in "observational learning" and imitation. In R. Glaser (Ed.), *The Nature of reinforcement.* New York: Academic Press, 1971. Pp. 279–309.

Glaser, R. Individuals and learning: The new aptitudes. *Educational Researcher*, 1972, *1*(6), 5–13.

Glass, G. V., Willson, V. L., & Gottman, J. M. Design and analysis of time-series experiments. Boulder, Colorado: Laboratory of Education Research, University of Colorado, 1972.

Glynn, E. L. Classroom applications of self-determined reinforcement. *Journal of Applied Behavior Analysis*, 1970, *3*, 123–132.

Gold, S., & Neufeld, I. L. A learning approach to the treatment of homosexuality. *Behaviour Research and Therapy*, 1965, *2*, 201–204.

Goldfried, M. R. Systematic desensitization as training in self-control. *Journal of Consulting and Clinical Psychology*, 1971, *37*(2), 228–234.

Goldiamond, I. Self-control procedures in personal behavior problems. *Psychological Reports*, 1965, *17*, 851–868. (a)

Goldiamond, I. Stuttering and fluency as manipulatable operant response classes. In L. Krasner & L. P. Ullmann (Eds.), *Research in behavior modification*. New York: Holt, Rinehart and Winston, Inc., 1965. Pp. 106–156. (b)

Goldstein, K. M. Note: A comparison of self- and peer-reports of smoking and drinking behavior. *Psychological Reports*, 1966, *18*, 702.

Goodlet, G. R., & Goodlet, M. M. Efficiency of self-monitored and externally imposed schedules of reinforcement in controlling disruptive behavior. Unpublished manuscript, University of Guelph, Ontario, 1969.

Gordon, S. B., & Sachs, L. B. Self-control with a covert aversive stimulus: Modification of smoking. Unpublished manuscript, West Virginia University, 1971.

Gottman, J. M. *N*-of-one and *N*-of-two research in psychotherapy. *Psychological Bulletin*, 1973, *80*, 93–105.

Gottman, J. M., & McFall, R. M. Self-monitoring effects in a program for potential high school dropouts: A time-series analysis. *Journal of Consulting and Clinical Psychology*, 1972, *39*, 273–281.

Grusec, J. Some antecedents of self-criticism. *Journal of Personality and Social Psychology*, 1966, *4*, 244–252.

Gustaitis, R. *Turning on*. New York: Macmillan, 1969.

Gutmann, M., & Marston, A. Problems of *S*'s motivation in behavioral program for reduction of cigarette smoking. *Psychological Reports*, 1967, *20*, 1107–1114.

Hagen, R. L. Group therapy versus bibliotherapy in weight reduction. Unpublished doctoral dissertation, University of Illinois, 1970.

Hall, S. M. Self-control and therapist control in the behavioral treatment of overweight women. *Behaviour Research and Therapy*, 1972, *10*, 59–68.

Hannum, J. W. The modification of evaluative self-thoughts and their effect on overt behavior. Unpublished doctoral dissertation, Stanford University, 1972.

Hannum, J. W., Thoresen, C. E., & Hubbard, D. R., Jr. A behavioral study of self-esteem with elementary teachers. In M. J. Mahoney & C. E. Thoresen, *Self-control: Power to the person*. Monterey, Calif.: Brooks-Cole, 1974.

Harris, M. B. Self-directed program for weight control: A pilot study. *Journal of Abnormal Psychology*, 1969, *74*, 263–270.

Hauck, L. P., & Martin, P. L. Music as a reinforcer in patient-controlled duration of time-out. *Journal of Music Therapy*, 1970, *7*, 43–53.

Haynes, L. E., & Kanfer, F. H. Academic rank, task feedback and self-reinforcement in children. *Psychological Reports*, 1971, *28*, 967–974.

Hefferline, R. F., & Bruno, L. J. J. The psychophysiology of private events. In A. Jacobs & L. Sachs (Eds.), *The psychology of private events.* New York: Academic Press, 1971. Pp. 163–192.

Helmstadter, G. C. *Research concepts in human behavior.* New York: Appleton, 1970.

Hendricks, C. G., Thoresen, C. E., & Hubbard, D. R., Jr. The effects of behavioral self-observation training on elementary teachers. Unpublished manuscript, Stanford University, 1973.

Herbert, E. W., & Baer, D. M. Training parents as behavior modifiers: Self-recording of contingent attention. *Journal of Applied Behavior Analysis*, 1972, *5*, 139–149.

Herbert, E. W., Gelfand, D. M., & Hartmann, D. P. Imitation and self-esteem as determinants of self-critical behavior. *Child Development*, 1969, *40*, 421–430.

Hilgard, E. R. Pain as a puzzle for psychology and physiology. *American Psychologist*, 1969, *24*, 103–113.

Hill, J. H., & Liebert, R. M. Effects of consistent or deviant modeling cues on the adoption of a self-imposed standard. *Psychonomic Science*, 1968, *13*, 243–244.

Hill, W. F. Learning theory and the acquisition of values. *Psychological Review*, 1960, *67*, 317–331.

Homme, L. E. Perspectives in psychology, XXIV: Control of coverants, the operants of the mind. *Psychological Record*, 1965, *15*, 501–511.

Horan, J. J., & Johnson, R. G. Coverant conditioning through self-management application of the Premack principle: Its effect on weight reduction. *Journal of Behavior Therapy and Experimental Psychiatry*, 1971, *2*, 243–249.

Houts, P., & Serber, M. (Eds.) *After the turn-on, what?* Champaign, Ill.: Research Press, 1972.

Jacks, R. Systematic desensitization compared with a self-management paradigm. Unpublished doctoral dissertation, Stanford University, 1972.

Jackson, B. Treatment of depression by self-reinforcement. *Behavior Therapy*, 1972, *3*, 298–307.

Jackson, B., & Van Zoost, B. Changing study behaviors through reinforcement contingencies. *Journal of Counseling Psychology*, 1972, *19*, 192–195.

Jeffrey, D. B. Self-regulation: A review and evaluation of research methodology for clinical applications. In M. J. Mahoney & C. E. Thoresen, *Self-control: Power to the person.* Monterey, Calif.: Brooks-Cole, 1974.

Jeffrey, D. B., Christensen, E. R., & Pappas, J. P. A case study report of a behavioral modification weight reduction group: Treatment and follow-up. Paper presented at the Rocky Mountain Psychological Association, Albuquerque, New Mexico, 1972.

Johnson, S. M. Self-reinforcement versus external reinforcement in behavior modification with children. *Developmental Psychology*, 1970, *3*, 147–148.

Johnson, S. M., & Martin, S. Developing self-evaluation as a conditioned reinforcer. In B. Ashem & E. G. Poser (Eds.), *Behavior modification with children*. New York: Pergamon, in press.

Johnson, S. M., & White, G. Self-observation as an agent of behavioral change. *Behavior Therapy*, 1971, *2*, 488–497.

Johnson, W. G. Some applications of Homme's coverant control therapy: Two case reports. *Behavior Therapy*, 1971, *2*, 240–248.

Kagan, N. *Influencing human interaction*. East Lansing, Mich.: Instructional Media Center, Michigan State University, 1972.

Kahn, M., & Baker, B. Desensitization with minimal therapist contact. *Journal of Abnormal Psychology*, 1968, *73*, 198–200.

Kamiya, J., Barber, T. X., DiCara, L. V., Miller, N. E., Shapiro, D., & Stoyva, J. (Eds.), *Biofeedback and self-control*. Chicago: Aldine-Atherton, 1971.

Kanfer, F. H. Self-reinforcement following operant lever pressing. Unpublished manuscript, University of Oregon, 1964.

Kanfer, F. H. Influence of age and incentive conditions on children as self-rewards. *Psychological Reports*, 1966, *19*, 263–274.

Kanfer, F. H. Self-monitoring: Methodological limitations and clinical applications. *Journal of Consulting and Clinical Psychology*, 1970, *35*, 148–152. (a)

Kanfer, F. H. Self-regulation: Research, issues and speculations. In C. Neuringer & J. L. Michael (Eds.), *Behavior modification in clinical psychology*. New York: Appleton, 1970. Pp. 178–220. (b)

Kanfer, F. H. The maintenance of behavior by self-generated stimuli and reinforcement. In A. Jacobs & L. B. Sachs (Eds.), *The psychology of private events: Perspectives on covert response systems*. New York: Academic Press, 1971. Pp. 39–59.

Kanfer, F. H. Behavior modification: An overview. In C. E. Thoresen (Ed.), *Behavior modification in education*. Seventy-Second Yearbook of the National Society for the Study of Education, Part I. Chicago: University of Chicago Press, 1973. Pp. 3–40.

Kanfer, F. H., Bradley, M. M., & Marston, A. R. Self-reinforcement as a function of degree of learning. *Psychological Reports*, 1962, *10*, 885–886.

Kanfer, F. H., Cox, L. E., Greiner, J. M., & Karoly, P. Contracts, demand characteristics and self-control. Unpublished manuscript, University of Cincinnati, 1972.

Kanfer, F. H., & Duerfeldt, P. H. Effects of pretraining on self-evaluation and self-reinforcement. *Journal of Personality and Social Psychology*, 1967, *2*, 164–168. (a)

Kanfer, F. H., & Duerfeldt, P. H. Effects on retention of externally or self-reinforced rehearsal trials following acquisition. *Psychological Reports*, 1967, *21*, 194–196. (b)

Kanfer, F. H., & Duerfeldt, P. H. Motivational properties of self-reinforcement. *Perceptual and Motor Skills*, 1967, *25*, 237–246. (c)

Kanfer, F. H., & Duerfeldt, P. H. Learner competence, model competence, and number of observation trials in vicarious learning. *Journal of Experimental Psychology*, 1967, *58*(3), 153–157. (d)

Kanfer, F. H., & Duerfeldt, P. H. Age, class standing, and commitment as determinants of cheating in children. *Child Development*, 1968, *39*, 545–557. (a)

Kanfer, F. H., & Duerfeldt, P. H. Comparison of self-reward and self-criticism as a function of types of prior external reinforcement. *Journal of Personality and Social Psychology*, 1968, *8*, 261–268. (b)

Kanfer, F. H., Duerfeldt, P. H., & LePage, A. L. Stability of patterns of self-reinforcement. *Psychological Reports*, 1969, *24*, 663–670.

Kanfer, F. H., & Goldfoot, D. A. Self-control and tolerance of noxious stimulation. *Psychological Reports*, 1966, *18*, 79–85.

Kanfer, F. H., & Karoly, P. Self-control: A behavioristic excursion into the lion's den. *Behavior Therapy*, 1972, *3*, 398–416. (a)

Kanfer, F. H., & Karoly, P. Self-regulation and its clinical application: Some additional conceptualizations. In R. C. Johnson, P. R. Dokecki, & O. H. Mowrer (Eds.), *Conscience, contract, and social reality*. New York: Holt, Rinehart and Winston, Inc., 1972. Pp. 428–437. (b)

Kanfer, F. H., & Marston, A. R. Determinants of self-reinforcement in human learning. *Journal of Experimental Psychology*, 1963, *66*, 245–254. (a)

Kanfer, F. H., & Marston, A. R. Conditioning of self-reinforcing responses: An analogue to self-confidence training. *Psychological Reports*, 1963, *13*, 63–70. (b)

Kanfer, F. H., & Phillips, J. S. Behavior therapy: A panacea for all ills or a passing fancy? *Archives of General Psychiatry*, 1966, *5*, 114–128.

Kanfer, F. H., & Phillips, J. S. *Learning foundations of behavior therapy*. New York: Wiley, 1970.

Kanfer, F. H., & Seidner, M. L. Self-control: Factors enhancing tolerance of noxious stimulation. *Journal of Personality and Social Psychology*, 1972, *39*, 370–380.

Kaplan, A. *The conduct of inquiry: Methodology for behavioral science*. Scranton: Chandler, 1964.

Kaufman, A., Baron, A., & Kopp, R. E. Some effects of instructions on human operant behavior. *Psychonomic Monograph Supplements*, 1966, *1*, 243–250.

Kaufman, K. F., & O'Leary, K. D. Reward, cost, and self-evaluation procedures for disruptive adolescents in a psychiatric hospital. *Journal of Applied Behavior Analysis*, 1972, *5*, 293–309.

Kazdin, A. E. Response cost: The removal of conditioned reinforcers for therapeutic change. *Behavior Therapy*, 1972, *3*, 533–546.

Kazdin, A. E. Self-monitoring and behavior change. In M. J. Mahoney & C. E. Thoresen, *Self-control: Power to the person*. Monterey, Calif.: Brooks-Cole, 1974.

Kelly, G. *The psychology of personal constructs*, Vol. 2. New York: Norton, 1955.

Keutzer, C. S. Behavior modification of smoking: The experimental investigation of diverse techniques. *Behaviour Research and Therapy*, 1968, *6*, 137–157.

Koch, S. Psychology cannot be a coherent science. *Psychology Today*, 1969, *3* (Sept.), 14ff.

Kohlberg, L. Stage and sequence: The cognitive-developmental approach to socialization. In D. Goslin (Ed.), *Handbook of socialization theory and research*. Chicago: Rand McNally, 1969.

Kolb, D. A., Winter, S. K., & Berlew, D. E. Self-directed change: Two studies. *Journal of Applied Behavior Science*, 1968, *4*, 453–471.

Kolvin, I. "Aversive imagery" treatment in adolescents. *Behaviour Research and Therapy*, 1967, *5*, 245–248.

Kopel, S. Some new perspectives on self-control. Paper presented at the Northwestern Association for the Advancement of Behavior Therapy, Seattle, May 1972.

Krop, H., Calhoon, B., & Verrier, R. Modification of the "self-concept" of emotionally disturbed children by covert reinforcement. *Behavior Therapy*, 1971, *2*, 617–624.

Krumboltz, J. D., & Thoresen, C. E. *Behavioral counseling: Cases and techniques*. New York: Holt, Rinehart and Winston, Inc., 1969.

Kunzelmann, H. D. (Ed.) *Precision teaching*. Seattle: Special Child Publications, 1970.

Lawson, D. M., & May, R. B. Three procedures for the extinction of smoking behavior. *Psychological Record*, 1970, *20*, 151–157.

Lazarus, A. A. New methods in psychotherapy: A case study. *South African Medical Journal*, 1958, *32*, 660–663.

Lazarus, A. A. Reflection on behavior therapy and its development: A point of view. *Behavior Therapy*, 1971, *2*, 369–374. (a)

Lazarus, A. A. *Behavior therapy and beyond*. New York: McGraw-Hill, 1971. (b)

Lazarus, A. A., & Davison, G. C. Clinical innovation in research and practice. In A. E. Bergin & S. L. Garfield (Eds.), *Handbook of psychotherapy and behavior change*. New York: Wiley, 1971. Pp. 196–213.

Lefcourt, H. M. Internal versus external control of reinforcement: A review. *Psychological Bulletin*, 1966, *65*, 206–220.

Leitenberg, H., Agras, W. S., Thompson, L. E., & Wright, D. E. Feedback in behavior modification: An experimental analysis in two phobic cases. *Journal of Applied Behavior Analysis*, 1968, *1*, 131–137.

Lesh, T. V. Zen meditation and the development of empathy in counselors. *Journal of Humanistic Psychology*, 1970, *10*, 39–74.

Levine, C. A conceptual analysis of self-control models. Unpublished manuscript, Pennsylvania State University, 1973.

Levinson, B. L., Shapiro, D., Schwartz, G. E., & Tursky, B. Smoking elimination by gradual reduction. *Behavior Therapy*, 1971, *2*, 477–487.

Liberman, R. P. Learning interpersonal skills in groups: Harnessing the behaviorist horse to the humanistic wagon. In P. Houts & M. Serber (Eds.), *After the turn-on, what?* Champaign, Ill.: Research Press, 1972. Pp. 89–109.

Lichtenstein, E., & Keutzer, C. S. Experimental investigation of diverse techniques to modify smoking: A follow-up report. *Behaviour Research and Therapy*, 1969, *7*, 139–140.

Liebert, R. M., & Allen, M. K. Effects of rule structure and reward magnitude on the acquisition and adoption of self-reward criteria. *Psychological Reports*, 1967, *21*, 445–452.

Liebert, R. M., Hanratty, M., & Hill, J. H. Effects of rule structure and training method on the adoption of a self-imposed standard. *Child Development*, 1969, *40*, 93–101.

Liebert, R. M., & Ora, J. P. Children's adoption of self-reward patterns: Incentive level and method of transmission. *Child Development*, 1968, *39*, 537–544.

Liebert, R. M., Spiegler, M. D., & Hall, W. M. Effects of the value of contingent self-administered and noncontingent externally imposed reward on children's behavioral productivity. *Psychonomic Science*, 1970, *18*, 245–246.

Lindsley, O. R. A reliable wrist counter for recording behavior rates. *Journal of Applied Behavior Analysis*, 1968, *1*, 77–78.

Locke, E. A., Cartledge, N., & Koeppel, J. Motivational effects of knowledge of results: A goal-setting phenomenon? *Psychological Bulletin*, 1968, *70*, 474–485.

Lovaas, O. I., Freitag, G., Gold, V. J., & Kassorla, I. C. Experimental studies in childhood schizophrenia: Analysis of self-destructive behavior. *Journal of Experimental Child Psychology*, 1965, *2*, 67–84.

Lovitt, T. C. Self-management projects with children. Unpublished manuscript, University of Washington, 1969.

Lovitt, T. C., & Curtiss, K. Academic response rate as a function of teacher- and self-imposed contingencies. *Journal of Applied Behavior Analysis*, 1969, *2*, 49–53.

Luria, A. R. *The role of speech in the regulation of normal and abnormal behavior.* New York: Liveright, 1961.

Luthe, W. *Autogenic training: Research and theory.* New York: Grune & Stratton, 1970.

Mahoney, M. J. Toward an experimental analysis of coverant control. *Behavior Therapy*, 1970, *1*, 510–521.

Mahoney, M. J. The self-management of covert behavior: A case study. *Behavior Therapy*, 1971, *2*, 575–578.

Mahoney, M. J. Research issues in self-management. *Behavior Therapy*, 1972, *3*, 45–63. (a)

Mahoney, M. J. Self-control strategies in weight loss. Paper presented at the Sixth Annual Meeting of the Association for the Advancement of Behavior Therapy, New York City, October 1972. (b)

Mahoney, M. J. Self-reward and self-monitoring techniques for weight control. *Behavior Therapy*, in press.

Mahoney, M. J., & Bandura, A. Self-reinforcement in pigeons. *Learning Motivation*, 1972, *3*, 293–303.

Mahoney, M. J., Bandura, A., Dirks, S. J., & Wright, C. L. Relative preference for external and self-controlled reinforcement in monkeys. Unpublished manuscript, Stanford University, 1973.

Mahoney, M. J., Moore, B. S., Wade, T. C., & Moura, N. G. M. The effects of continuous and intermittent self-monitoring on academic behavior. *Journal of Consulting and Clinical Psychology*, 1973, *41*, 65–69.

Mahoney, M. J., Moura, N. G. M., & Wade, T. C. The relative efficacy of self-reward, self-punishment, and self-monitoring techniques for weight loss. *Journal of Consulting and Clinical Psychology*, 1973, *40*, 404–407.

Mahoney, M. J., & Thoresen, C. E. *Self-control: Power to the person.* Monterey, Calif.: Brooks-Cole, 1974.

Mahoney, M. J., Thoresen, C. E., & Danaher, B. G. Covert behavior modification: An experimental analogue. *Journal of Behavior Therapy and Experimental Psychiatry*, 1972, *3*, 7–14.

Maltz, M. *Psycho-cybernetics.* Englewood Cliffs, N.J.: Prentice-Hall, 1960.

Mann, R. A. The behavior-therapeutic use of contingency contracting to control an adult behavior problem: Weight control. *Journal of Applied Behavior Analysis*, 1972, *5*, 99–109.

Manno, B., & Marston, A. R. Weight reduction as a function of negative covert reinforcement (sensitization) versus positive covert reinforcement. *Behaviour Research and Therapy*, 1972, *10*, 201–207.

Marquis, J. N. Orgasmic reconditioning: Changing sexual object choice through controlling masturbation fantasies. *Journal of Behavior Therapy and Experimental Psychiatry*, 1970, *1*, 263–272.

Marquis, J. N., & Morgan, W. G. *A guidebook for systematic desensitization.* Veteran's Administration Hospital, Palo Alto, Calif., 1968.

Marston, A. R. Personality variables related to self-reinforcement. *Journal of Psychology*, 1964, *58*, 169–175. (a)

Marston, A. R. Response strength and self-reinforcement. *Journal of Experimental Psychology*, 1964, *68*, 537–540. (b)

Marston, A. R. Variables affecting incidence of self-reinforcement. *Psychological Reports*, 1964, *14*, 879–884. (c)

Marston, A. R. Imitation, self-reinforcement, and reinforcement of another person. *Journal of Personality and Social Psychology*, 1965, *2*, 255–261.

Marston, A. R. Self-reinforcement and external reinforcement in visual-motor learning. *Journal of Experimental Psychology*, 1967, *74*, 93–98.

Marston, A. R. Dealing with low self-confidence. *Educational Research*, 1968, *10*, 134–138.

Marston, A. R. Effect of external feedback on the rate of positive self-reinforcement. *Journal of Experimental Psychology*, 1969, *80*, 175–179.

Marston, A. R., & Cohen, N. J. The relationship of negative self-reinforcement to frustration and intropunitiveness. *Journal of General Psychology*, 1966, *74*, 237–243.

Marston, A. R., & Feldman, S. F. Toward the use of self-control in behavior modification. *Journal of Consulting and Clinical Psychology*, 1972, *39*(1), 329–433.

Marston, A. R., & Kanfer, F. H. Human reinforcement: Experimenter and subject controlled. *Journal of Experimental Psychology*, 1963, *66*, 91–94.

Marston, A. R., & Smith, F. J. Relationship between reinforcement of another person and self-reinforcement. *Psychological Reports*, 1968, *22*, 83–90.

Maslow, A. H. *The psychology of science.* New York: Harper & Row, 1966.

Maslow, A. H. Toward a humanistic biology. *American Psychologist*, 1969, *24*, 724–735.

Matson, F. W. *The broken image.* New York: Braziller, 1964.

Matson, F. W. Matson replies to Skinner. *Humanist*, 1971, *31*, 2.

May, R. *Love and will.* New York: Norton, 1969.

McFall, R. M. The effects of self-monitoring on normal smoking behavior. *Journal of Consulting and Clinical Psychology*, 1970, *35*, 135–142.

McFall, R. M., & Hammen, C. L. Motivation, structure, and self-monitoring: The role of nonspecific factors in smoking reduction. *Journal of Consulting and Clinical Psychology*, 1972, *37*, 80–86.

McGuire, R. J., & Vallance, M. Aversion therapy by electric shock: A simple technique. *British Medical Journal*, 1964, *1*, 151–153.

McMains, M. J., & Liebert, R. M. Influence of discrepancies between successively modeled self-reward criteria on the adoption of a self-imposed standard. *Journal of Personality and Social Psychology*, 1968, *8*, 166–171.

McMains, M. J., Liebert, R. M., Hill, J. H., Spiegler, M. D., & Baker, E. L. Children's adoption of self-reward patterns: Verbalization and modeling. *Perceptual and Motor Skills*, 1969, *28*, 515–518.

McNamara, J. R. Systematic desensitization versus implosive therapy: Issues in outcomes. *Psychotherapy: Theory, Research, and Practice*, 1972, *9*, 13–16.

Mees, H. L. Sadistic fantasies modified by aversive conditioning and substitution. *Behaviour Research and Therapy*, 1966, *4*, 317–320. (a)

Mees, H. L. Placebo effects in aversive control: A preliminary report. Paper read at joint Oregon-Washington State Psychological Association, Ocean Shores, Washington, 1966. (b)

Meichenbaum, D. H. Cognitive factors in behavior modification: Modifying what clients say to themselves. Paper presented at the Fifth Annual Meeting of the Association for the Advancement of Behavior Therapy, Washington, D.C., September 1971.

Meichenbaum, D. H., & Cameron, R. The clinical potential and pitfalls of modifying what clients say to themselves. In M. J. Mahoney & C. E. Thoresen, *Self-control: Power to the person*. Monterey, Calif., 1974.

Meichenbaum, D. H., Gilmore, J. B., & Fedoravicius, A. Group insight versus group desensitization in treating speech anxiety. *Journal of Consulting and Clinical Psychology*, 1971, *36*, 410–421.

Meichenbaum, D. H. & Goodman, J. Training impulsive children to talk to themselves: A means for developing self-control. *Journal of Abnormal Psychology*, 1971, *77*, 115–126.

Menefee, M., & Thoresen, C. E. Effects of modeling and self-control treatments in reducing fear of heights. Unpublished manuscript, Stanford University, 1973.

Migler, B., & Wolpe, J. Automated self-desensitization: A case report. *Behaviour Research and Therapy*, 1967, *5*, 133–135.

Miller, G. A., Galanter, E., & Pribram, K. H. *Plans and the structure of behavior*. New York: Holt, Rinehart and Winston, Inc., 1960.

Miller, M. M. Treatment of chronic alcoholism by hypnotic aversion. *Journal of the American Medical Association*, 1959, *171*, 1492–1495.

Miller, N. E. Learning of visceral and glandular responses. *Science*, 1969, *163*, 434–453.

Miller, P. M. The use of behavioral contracting in the treatment of alcoholism: A case report. *Behavior Therapy*, 1972, *3*, 593–596.

Mischel, W. *Personality and assessment.* New York: Wiley, 1968.

Mischel, W. *Introduction to personality.* New York: Holt, Rinehart and Winston, Inc., 1971.

Mischel, W. Toward a cognitive social learning reconceptualization of personality. *Psychological Review,* 1973, *80,* 252–283.

Mischel, W., Ebbesen, E. B., & Zeiss, A. R. Cognitive and attentional mechanisms in delay of gratification. *Journal of Personality and Social Psychology,* 1972, *21,* 204–218.

Mischel, W., Ebbesen, E. B., & Zeiss, A. R. Selective attention to the self: Situational and dispositional determinants. *Journal of Personality and Social Psychology,* in press.

Mischel, W., & Gilligan, C. Delay of gratification, motivation for the prohibited gratification, and responses to temptation. *Journal of Abnormal and Social Psychology,* 1964, *69,* 411–417.

Mischel, W., & Liebert, R. M. Effects of discrepancies between observed and imposed reward criteria on their acquisition and transmission. *Journal of Personality and Social Psychology,* 1966, *3,* 45–53.

Mischel, W., & Liebert, R. M. The role of power in the adoption of self-reward patterns. *Child Development,* 1967, *38,* 673–683.

Mischel, W., & Masters, J. C. Effects of probability of reward attainment on responses to frustration. *Journal of Personality and Social Psychology,* 1966, *3,* 390–396.

Mischel, W., & Metzner, R. Preference for delayed reward as a function of age, intelligence, and length of delay interval. *Journal of Abnormal and Social Psychology,* 1962, *64,* 425–431.

Mischel, W., & Staub, E. Effects of expectancy on working and waiting for larger rewards. *Journal of Personality and Social Psychology,* 1965, *2,* 625–643.

Montgomery, G. T., & Parton, D. H. Reinforcing effect of self-reward. *Journal of Experimental Psychology,* 1970, *84,* 273–276.

Moore, F. J., Chernell, E., & West, M. J. Television as a therapeutic tool. *Archives of General Psychiatry,* 1965, *12*(2), 117–120.

Morgan, W. G., & Bass, B. A. Self-control through self-mediated rewards. Paper presented at the Fifth Annual Meeting of the Association for the Advancement of Behavior Therapy, Washington, D.C., September 1971.

Morganstern, K. P. Implosive therapy and flooding procedures. *Psychological Bulletin,* 1973, *79,* 318–334.

Morganstern, K. P. Cigarette smoke as a noxious stimulus in self-managed aversion therapy for compulsive eaters. *Behavior Therapy,* in press.

Nagel, E. *The structure of science: Problems in the logic of scientific explanation.* New York: Harcourt, 1961.

Neisser, U. *Cognitive psychology.* New York: Appleton, 1967.

Neisworth, J. T. Elimination of cigarette smoking through gradual phase-out of stimulus controls. *Behaviorally Speaking*, 1972, Oct., 1–3.

Nelson, C. M., & McReynolds, T. Self-recording and control behavior: A reply to Simkins. *Behavior Therapy*, 1971, 2, 494–497.

Nisbett, R. E., & Valins, S. *Perceiving the causes of one's own behavior.* New York: General Learning Press, 1971.

Nolan, J. D. Self-control procedures in the modification of smoking behavior. *Journal of Consulting and Clinical Psychology*, 1968, 32, 92–93.

Ober, D. C. Modification of smoking behavior. *Journal of Consulting and Clinical Psychology*, 1968, 32, 543–549.

O'Leary, K. D. The effects of self-instruction on immoral behavior. *Journal of Experimental Child Psychology*, 1968, 6, 297–301.

Orne, M. T. On the social psychology of the psychological experiment: With particular reference to demand characteristics and their implications. *American Psychologist*, 1962, 17, 776–783.

Orne, M. T. From the subject's point of view, when is behavior private and when is it public?: Problems of inference. *Journal of Consulting and Clinical Psychology*, 1970, 35, 143–147.

Paivio, A., Mental imagery—associative learning and memory. *Psychological Review*, 1969, 76, 241–263.

Patterson, G. R. Reprogramming the families of aggressive boys. In C. E. Thoresen (Ed.), *Behavior modification in education.* Seventy-Second Yearbook of the National Society for the Study of Education, Part I. Chicago: University of Chicago Press, 1973. Pp. 154–192.

Peale, N. V. *The power of positive thinking.* Englewood Cliffs, N.J.: Prentice-Hall, 1960.

Penick, S. B., Filion, R., Fox, S., & Stunkard, A. J. Behavior modification in the treatment of obesity. *Psychosomatic Medicine*, 1971, 33, 49–55.

Phillips, R. E., Johnson, G. D., & Geyer, A. Self-administered systematic desensitization. *Behaviour Research and Therapy*, 1972, 10, 93–96.

Powell, J. R., & Azrin, N. The effects of shock as a punisher for cigarette smoking. *Journal of Applied Behavior Analysis*, 1968, 1, 63–71.

Premack, D. Reinforcement theory. In D. Levin (Ed.), *Nebraska symposium on motivation: 1965.* Lincoln, Neb.: University of Nebraska Press, 1965. Pp. 123–180.

Premack, D. Mechanisms of self-control. In W. A. Hunt (Ed.), *Learning and mechanisms of control of smoking.* Chicago: Aldine-Atherton, 1970. Pp. 107–123.

Premack, D. Catching up with common sense or two sides of a generalization: Reinforcement and punishment. In R. Glaser (Ed.), *The nature of reinforcement.* New York: Academic Press, 1971. Pp. 121–150.

Premack, D. How to socialize a rat: On the possibilities of self-control in man and animals. Paper presented at the American Cancer Society meeting, Tucson, Arizona, 1972.

Rachlin, H. *Introduction to modern behaviorism.* San Francisco: Freeman, 1970.

Rachlin, H., & Green, L. Delay of gratification as simple choice. Unpublished manuscript, State University of New York at Stony Brook, 1972.

Rachman, S., & Teasdale, A. *Aversion therapy and behavior disorders: An analysis.* Coral Gables, Fla.: University of Miami Press, 1969.

Rehm, L. P., & Marston, A. R. Reduction of social anxiety through modification of self-reinforcement: An instigation therapy technique. *Journal of Consulting and Clinical Psychology*, 1968, *32*, 565–574.

Reid, J. B. Reliability assessment of observation data: A possible methodological problem. *Child Development*, 1970, *41*, 1143–1150.

Risley, T. R., & Hart, B. Developing correspondence between the nonverbal and verbal behavior of preschool children. *Journal of Applied Behavior Analysis*, 1968, *1*, 267–281.

Roberts, A. H. Self-control procedures in modification of smoking behavior: Replication. *Psychological Reports*, 1969, *24*, 675–676.

Rogers, C. *On becoming a person.* Boston: Houghton Mifflin, 1961.

Rosenhan, D., Frederick, F., & Burrowes, A. Preaching and practicing: Effects of channel discrepancy on norm internalization. *Child Development*, 1968, *39*, 291–301.

Rosenthal, R. *Experimenter effects in behavioral research.* New York: Appleton, 1966.

Rosenthal, R. Covert communication in the psychological experiment. *Psychological Bulletin*, 1967, *67*, 356–367.

Roszak, T. *The making of a counter culture: Reflections on the technocratic society and its youthful opposition.* Garden City, N.Y.: Doubleday, 1969.

Rotter, J. B., Chance, J. E., & Phares, E. J. (Eds.), *Applications of a social learning theory of personality.* New York: Holt, Rinehart and Winston, Inc., 1972.

Rubin, R. D., Merbaum, M., & Fried, R. Self-imposed punishment versus desensitization. In R. D. Rubin, H. Fensterheim, A. A. Lazarus, & C. M. Franks (Eds.), *Advances in behavior therapy* (Vol. 3). New York: Academic Press, 1971. Pp. 85–91.

Rutner, I. T. The modification of smoking behavior through techniques of self-control. Unpublished master's thesis, Wichita State University, 1967.

Rutner, I. T., & Bugle, C. An experimental procedure for the modification of psychotic behavior. *Journal of Consulting and Clinical Psychology*, 1969, *33*, 651–653.

Sachs, L. B. Construing hypnosis as modifiable behavior. In A. Jacobs & L. B. Sachs (Eds.), *The psychology of private events.* New York: Academic Press, 1971. Pp. 62–75.

Sachs, L. B., Bean, H., & Morrow, J. E. Comparison of smoking treatments. *Behavior Therapy*, 1970, *1*, 465–472.

Sandler, J. Masochism: An empirical analysis. *Psychological Bulletin*, 1964, *62*, 197–204.

Sandler, J., & Quagliano, J. Punishment in a signal avoidance situation. Paper presented at the Southeastern Psychological Association, Gatlinburg, Tennessee, 1964.

Schachter, S. The interaction of cognitive and physiological determinants of emotional state. In C. D. Speilberger (Ed.), *Anxiety and behavior*. New York: Academic Press, 1966.

Schaefer, H. H. Self-injurious behavior: Shaping "head-banging" in monkeys. *Journal of Applied Behavior Analysis*, 1970, *3*, 111–116.

Schultz, J. H., & Luthe, W. *Autogenic training*. New York: Grune & Stratton, 1959.

Seligman, M. E. P., & Maier, S. F. Failure to escape traumatic shock. *Journal of Experimental Psychology*, 1967, *74*, 1–9.

Shapiro, D., Barber, T. X., DiCara, L. V., Kamiya, J., Miller, N. E., & Stoyva, J. (Eds.), *Biofeedback and self-control*. Chicago: Aldine-Atherton, 1973.

Shapiro, D., Tursky, B., Schwartz, G. E., & Shnidman, S. R. Smoking on cue: A behavioral approach to smoking reduction. *Journal of Health and Social Behavior*, 1971, *12*, 108–113. Reprinted in M. J. Mahoney & C. E. Thoresen, *Self-control: Power to the person*. Monterey, Calif.: Brooks-Cole, 1974.

Sidman, M. *Tactics of scientific research: Evaluating experimental data in psychology*. New York: Basic Books, 1960.

Simkins, L. A rejoinder to Nelson and McReynolds on the self-recording of behavior. *Behavior Therapy*, 1971, *2*, 598–601. (a)

Simkins, L. The reliability of self-recorded behaviors. *Behavior Therapy*, 1971, *2*, 83–87. (b)

Skinner, B. F. *Science and human behavior*. New York: Macmillan, 1953.

Skinner, B. F. Behaviorism at fifty. *Science*, 1963, *140*, 951–958.

Skinner, B. F. *Contingencies of reinforcement: A theoretical analysis*. New York: Appleton, 1969.

Skinner, B. F. *Beyond freedom and dignity*. New York: Knopf, 1971.

Skinner, B. F. Some implications of making education more efficient. In C. E. Thoresen (Ed.), *Behavior modification in education*. Seventy-Second Yearbook of the National Society for the Study of Education, Part I. Chicago: University of Chicago Press, 1973, Pp. 446–456.

Spence, D. P. Analog and digital descriptions of behavior. *American Psychologist*, 1973, *28*, 479–488.

Staats, A. W. *Child learning, intelligence, and personality*. New York: Harper & Row, 1971.

Staats, A. W. Language behavior therapy: A derivative of social behaviorism. *Behavior Therapy*, 1972, *3*, 165–192.

Stampfl, T. G., & Levis, D. J. Essentials of implosive therapy: A learning-theory-based psychodynamic behavior-therapy. *Journal of Abnormal Psychology*, 1967, *72*, 496–503.

Staub, E. Effects of persuasion and modeling on delay of gratification. *Developmental Psychology*, 1972, *6*, 166–177.

Staub, E., & Kellet, D. S. Increasing pain tolerance by information about aversive stimuli. *Journal of Personality and Social Psychology*, 1972, *21*, 198–203.

Staub, E., Tursky, B., & Schwartz, G. E. Self-control and predictability: Their effects on reactions to aversive stimulation. *Journal of Personality and Social Psychology*, 1971, *18*, 157–162.

Steffy, R. A., Meichenbaum, D., & Best, A. Aversive and cognitive factors in the modification of smoking behavior. *Behaviour Research and Therapy*, 1970, *8*, 115–125.

Stein, A. H. Imitation of resistance to temptation. *Child Development*, 1967, *38*, 157–169.

Stoller, F. Accelerated interaction: A time-limited approach based on the brief, intensive group. *International Journal of Group Psychotherapy*, 1968, *18*(2), 220–258.

Stone, L. J., & Hokanson, J. E. Arousal reduction via self-punitive behavior. *Journal of Personality and Social Psychology*, 1969, *12*, 72–79.

Stotland, E., & Zander, A. Effects of public and private failure on self-evaluation. *Journal of Abnormal and Social Psychology*, 1958, *56*, 223–229.

Stoyva, J., Barber, T. X., DiCara, L. V., Kamiya, J., Miller, N. E., & Shapiro, D. (Eds.), *Biofeedback and self-control 1971*. Chicago: Aldine-Atherton, 1972.

Stuart, R. B. Behavioral control over eating. *Behaviour Research and Therapy*, 1967, *5*, 357–365.

Stuart, R. B. *Trick or treatment: How and when psychotherapy fails*. Champaign, Ill.: Research Press, 1970.

Stuart, R. B. A three-dimensional program for the treatment of obesity. *Behaviour Research and Therapy*, 1971, *9*, 177–186.

Stuart, R. B. Situational versus self-control. In R. D. Rubin, H. Fensterheim, J. D. Henderson, & L. P. Ullmann (Eds.), *Advances in behavior therapy*. New York: Academic Press, 1972. Pp. 129–146.

Stuart, R. B., & Davis, B. *Slim chance in a fat world: Behavioral control of obesity*. Champaign, Ill.: Research Press, 1972.

Stumphauzer, J. S. Behavior modification with juvenile delinquents: A critical review. *FCI Technical and Treatment Notes*, 1970, *1*, Whole No. 2. (a)

Stumphauzer, J. S. Modification of delay choices in institutionalized youthful offenders through social reinforcement. *Psychonomic Science*, 1970, *18*, 222–223. (b)

Stumphauzer, J. S. Increased delay of gratification in young prison inmates through imitation of high-delay peer models. *Journal of Personality and Social Psychology*, 1972, *21*, 10–17.

Stunkard, A. New therapies for the eating disorders: Behavior modification of obesity and anorexia nervosa. *Archives of General Psychiatry*, 1972, *26*, 391–398.

Suinn, R. M. The application of short-term videotape therapy for the treatment of test anxiety of college students. *Progress Report*, Colorado State University, December, 1970.

Suinn, R. M., & Richardson, I. Anxiety management training: A nonspecific behavior therapy program for anxiety control. *Behavior Therapy*, 1971, *2*, 498–510.

Sutich, A. J. Some considerations regarding transpersonal psychology. *Journal of Transpersonal Psychology*, 1969, *1*, 11–20.

Tart, C. T. States of consciousness and state-specific sciences. *Science*, 1972, *176*, 1203–1210.

Terrace, H. S. Awareness as viewed by conventional and by radical behaviorism. Paper presented at the Seventy-ninth American Psychological Association meeting, Washington, D.C., 1971.

Thelen, M. H. Modeling of verbal reactions of failure. *Developmental Psychology*, 1969, *1*, 297.

Thomas, D. R. Preliminary findings on self-monitoring for modifying teaching behaviors. In B. H. Hopkins (Ed.), *A new direction for education: Behavior analysis 1971* (Vol. 1). University of Kansas, 1971. Pp. 102–114.

Thomas, E. J., Abrams, K. S., & Johnson, J. B. Self-monitoring and reciprocal inhibition in the modification of multiple ties of Gilles De La Tourette's syndrome. *Journal of Behavior Therapy and Experimental Psychiatry*, 1971, *2*, 159–171.

Thoresen, C. E. Behavioral humanism. In C. E. Thoresen (Ed.), *Behavior modification in education*. Seventy-Second Yearbook of the National Society for the Study of Education, Part I. Chicago: University of Chicago Press, 1973. Pp. 385–421. (a)

Thoresen, C. E. Behavioral self-observation in reducing drinking behavior: A case study. Unpublished manuscript, Stanford University, 1973. (b)

Thoresen, C. E. The intensive design: An intimate approach to counseling research. *The Counseling Psychologist*, in press.

Thoresen, C. E., & Hosford, R. Behavioral approaches to counseling. In C. E. Thoresen (Ed.), *Behavior modification in education*. Seventy-second Yearbook of the National Society for the Study of Education. Chicago: University of Chicago Press, 1973.

Thoresen, C. E., Hubbard, D. R., Hannum, J. W., Hendricks, C. G., & Shapiro, D. Behavioral self-observation training with a nursery school teacher. Research and Development Memorandum No. 110, Stanford, Calif.: Stanford Center for Research and Development in Teaching, June 1973.

Thoresen, C. E., Hubbard, D. R., Hannum, J. W., Hendricks, C. G., & Shapiro, D. Reliability and reactivity of self-observation on a teacher's verbal praise. Research and Development Memorandum, Stanford, Calif.: Stanford Center for Research and Development in Teaching, in press.

Throop, W. F., & MacDonald, A. P. Internal-external locus of control: A bibliography. *Psychological Reports*, Monograph Supplement 1, *28*, 1971, 175–190.

Todd, F. J. Covariant control of self-evaluative responses in the treatment of depression: A new use for an old principle. *Behavior Therapy*, 1972, *3*, 91–94.

Todd, F. J., & Kelley, R. J. The use of hypnosis to facilitate conditioned relaxation responses: A report of three cases. *Journal of Behavior Therapy and Experimental Psychiatry*, 1970, *1*, 295–298.

Tooley, J. T., & Pratt, S. An experimental procedure for the extinction of smoking behavior. *Psychological Record*, 1967, *17*, 209–218.

Turner, M. B. *Philosophy and the science of behavior*. New York: Appleton, 1967.

Tyler, V. O., & Straughan, J. H. Coverant control and breath holding as techniques for the treatment of obesity. *Psychological Record*, 1970, *20*, 473–478.

Upper, D., & Meredith, L. A. A stimulus-control approach to the modification of smoking behavior. Paper presented at the Seventy-eighth American Psychological Association Convention, Miami, September 1970.

Upper, D., & Meredith, L. A. A timed interval procedure for modifying cigarette-smoking behavior. Unpublished manuscript, Brockton Veteran's Administration Hospital, Brockton, Mass., 1971.

Valins, S., & Nisbett, R. E. *Attribution processes in the development and treatment of emotional disorders*. New York: General Learning Press, 1971.

Voss, S. C., & Homzie, M. J. Choice as a value. *Psychological Reports*, 1970, *26*, 912–914.

Vygotsky, L. S. *Thought and language*. New York: Wiley, 1962.

Wagner, M. K., & Bragg, R. A. Comparing behavior modification approaches to habit decrement—smoking. *Journal of Consulting and Clinical Psychology*, 1970, *34*, 258–263.

Wahler, R. G. Setting generality: Some specific and general effects of child behavior therapy. *Journal of Applied Behavior Analysis*, 1969, *2*, 239–246.

Wallace, R. K. Physiological effects of transcendental meditation. *Science*, 1970, *167*, 1751–1754.

Walters, R. H., Leat, M., & Mezei, L. Inhibition and disinhibition of responses through empathetic learning. *Canadian Journal of Psychology*, 1963, *17*, 235–243.

Walters, R. H., & Parke, R. D. Influence of response consequences to a social model on resistance to deviation. *Journal of Experimental Child Psychology*, 1964, *1*, 269–280.

Walters, R. H., Parke, R. D., & Cane, V. A. Timing of punishment and the observation of consequences to others as determinants of response inhibition. *Journal of Experimental Child Psychology*, 1965, *2*, 10–30.

Walz, G. R., & Johnson, J. A. Counselors look at themselves on videotape. *Journal of Counseling Psychology*, 1963, *10*, 232–236.

Watts, A. *Psychotherapy east and west*. New York: Ballantine, 1961.

Webb, E. J., Campbell, D. T., Schwartz, R. D., & Sechrest, L. *Unobtrusive measures: Nonreactive research in the social sciences*. Chicago: Rand McNally, 1966.

Weiner, H. Real and imagined cost effects upon human fixed-internal responding. *Psychological Reports*, 1965, *17*, 659–662.

Weingartner, A. H. Self-administered aversive stimulation with hallucinating hospitalized schizophrenics. *Journal of Consulting and Clinical Psychology*, 1971, *36*, 422–429.

Whitehead, A. *Science and the modern world*. New York: Mentor Book, 1948 (original edition 1925).

Wisocki, P. Treatment of obsessive-compulsive behavior by covert sensitization and covert reinforcement: A case report. *Journal of Behavior Therapy and Experimental Psychiatry*, 1970, *1*, 233–239.

Wisocki, P., & Rooney, E. J. A comparison of thought-stopping and covert sensitization techniques in the treatment of smoking. Paper presented at the Fifth Annual Meeting of the Association for the Advancement of Behavior Therapy, Washington, D.C., September 1971.

Wolf, M. M., & Risley, T. R. Reinforcement: Applied research. In R. Glaser (Ed.), *The nature of reinforcement*. New York: Academic Press, 1971. Pp. 310–325.

Wollersheim, J. P. Effectiveness of group therapy based upon learning principles in the treatment of overweight women. *Journal of Abnormal Psychology*, 1970, *6*, 462–474.

Wolpe, J. *Psychotherapy by reciprocal inhibition*. Stanford, Calif.: Stanford University Press, 1958.

Wolpe, J. Conditioned inhibition of craving in drug addiction: A pilot experiment. *Behaviour Research and Therapy*, 1965, *2*, 285–288.

Yamagami, T. The treatment of an obsession by thought-stopping. *Journal of Behavior Therapy and Experimental Psychiatry*, 1971, *2*, 133–136.

Zeisset, R. M. Desensitization and relaxation in the modification of psychiatric patients' interview behavior. *Journal of Abnormal Psychology*, 1968, *73*, 18–24.

Name Index

Subject Index